147
SNOOKER
DRILLS AND EXERCISES

147 SNOOKER

DRILLS AND EXERCISES

Andrew Highfield and David Horrix

THE CROWOOD PRESS

First published in 2017 by
The Crowood Press Ltd
Ramsbury, Marlborough
Wiltshire SN8 2HR

enquiries@crowood.com
www.crowood.com

This impression 2025

British Library Cataloguing-in-Publication Data
A catalogue record for this book is available from the British Library.

For product safety-related questions, contact productsafety@crowood.com

ISBN 978 1 78500 355 4

Typeset by Nova Techset Private Limited, Bengaluru and Chennai
Printed and bound in india by Nutech Print Services

Contents

INTRODUCTION

The snooker player who wishes to improve and play at a high level must have the right tools to assist in their development. This book provides the drills and exercises that are used by professional coaches to develop players to their full potential. Packed with 147 of the most useful and beneficial exercises, this book will bring the structure to your practice sessions that you need to improve.

As well as being challenging the exercises are also fun to try, and many top players have benefited from challenging themselves and also, more importantly, enjoying their training.

147 Snooker Drills can be used by every standard of player, from beginner through to advanced player, as there are different targets dependent upon your current level of ability. The authors use the exercises in this book on a weekly basis and many players have benefited from improving their knowledge and understanding of how to play snooker through practising the exercises.

We hope you enjoy reading this book as much as we have enjoyed producing it, and if you practise the drills and exercises that are contained within the book we are confident that your knowledge of the game will improve significantly.

Andrew Highfield and David Horrix

K1

UP AND DOWN THE SPOTS

Aim at the chalk and back to the tip

Description

Place a chalk on the cushion in line with the black spot, place the cue ball on the brown spot and 2 reds behind the cue ball only showing a small segment in the centre. Aiming at the chalk, hit the cue ball over the 4 spots and back to the tip of your cue.

Why this Is a Good Exercise

1. Ensures straight cueing
2. Requires you to stay down on the shot
3. Develops touch

Practice Objectives – Over the Spots

Beginner	Complete once
Intermediate	Complete twice in succession
Advanced	Complete four times in succession

Coaching Top Tips and Trivia

Try to learn a little about the game of billiards and in your snooker practice also try to incorporate a few billiards shots. It's a superb way of learning angles and positional play and can be very relaxing and enjoyable.

K2

ROAD BLOCK COLOUR CLEARANCE

Clear the colours without touching the reds or the triangles

Description

Start from anywhere inside the D and aim to clear the colours in sequence. After potting the pink ball gain position on one of the reds either side of black then clear red, black and the final red.

At no point in the clearance must the cue ball touch any of the reds on the blue line or either of the triangles.

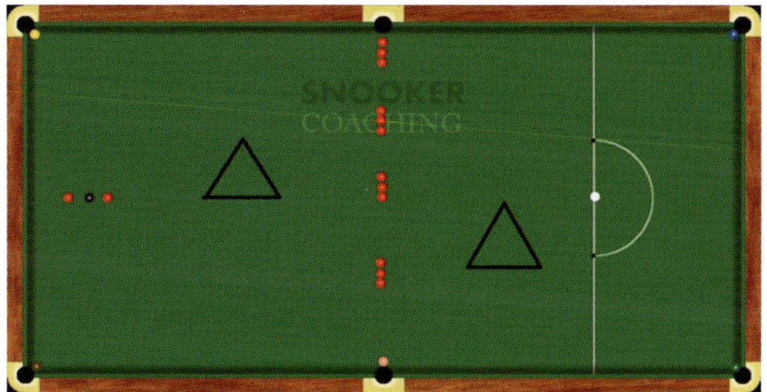

Why this Is a Good Exercise

1. Good control of the cue ball is needed
2. Improves positional play
3. Ensures you understand what you wish to achieve before going down on the shot.

Practice Objectives – For the Road Block Colour Clearance

Beginner   1 out of 10
Intermediate   3 out of 10
Advanced   8 out of 10

Coaching Top Tips and Trivia

To keep your snooker cue feeling silky smooth and in good condition put some beeswax onto a strip of 00000 grade steel wool. Rub the wool up and down the shaft and the steel wool removes any dirt or grease while the beeswax seals and nourishes the wood.

K3

UP AND DOWN AND CUE BETWEEN 2 REDS

Avoid hitting the reds

Description

Place a chalk on the cushion in line with the black spot, place the cue ball on the brown spot and 2 reds either side with just a few centimetres gap.

Aiming at the chalk hit the cue ball over the spots and back over the brown spot and into baulk.

Avoid any contact from white or cue with the reds.

Why this Is a Good Exercise

1. Requires a good aim
2. Encourages straight cueing
3. Improves control over the cue

Practice Objectives – Between 2 Reds

Beginner   3 out of 10
Intermediate   8 out of 10
Advanced   10 out of 10

Coaching Top Tips and Trivia

The quickest century break ever made in a tournament was done so by Tony Drago in just 3 minutes and 31 seconds – quite some going but Tony was quite some player!

K4

FEATHER TOUCH

Make contact with the red ball without potting the colour

Description

Place the balls as illustrated with both red and colour touching and just 1 inch from the pocket.

Starting from a straight line position in baulk aim to hit the cue ball very gently to hit red full in the face without potting yellow.

Once complete remove the red and yellow from the table and move on to green, brown, blue, pink and black.

Why this Is a Good Exercise

1. Helps develop superb touch
2. Requires concentration
3. Requires persistence

Practice Objectives – For the Feather Touch

Beginner   20 attempts on each set to make contact
Intermediate   10 attempts on each set to make contact
Advanced   3 attempts on each set to make contact

Coaching Top Tips and Trivia

Exert a little more pressure through the index finger of the bridge hand. This stabilizes the bridge and helps it to remain still when playing the shot.

K5

FULL BALL CANNON

Cannon red and white around pink spot

Description

Place a block of chalk as indicated. Hit the red ball on the blue spot full in the face sending it off the top cushion and back for a cannon with the white ball around about the pink spot.

Use a small amount of top spin for this shot.

Why this Is a Good Exercise

1. Requires straight cueing
2. Improves aiming
3. Requires perfect stillness on the shot

Practice Objectives – Full Ball Cannon

Beginner   Complete once only
Intermediate   Complete 3 times
Advanced   Complete 5 times

Coaching Top Tips and Trivia

The referee is allowed to inform a colour-blind player the colour of a specific ball if he is requested to do so by the player.

K6

3 REDS FOR AKANI

You believe you can control the cue ball?

Description

Set the balls as illustrated.

Starting from any position aim to pot a red (then re-spot the potted red) and gain position on one of the other reds. Continue like this aiming to make as many pots as possible in succession.

Note – you can't pot the same red twice in succession.

Easy?

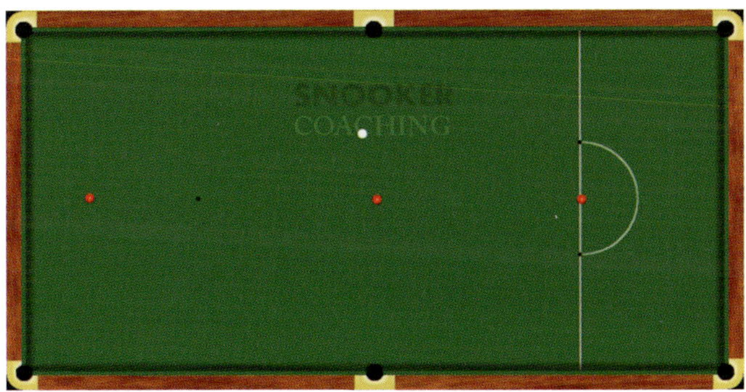

Why this Is a Good Exercise

1. Pinpoint accuracy and control is needed
2. Determination needed
3. This forces you to appraise how much control of the cue ball you really have

Practice Objectives – For 3 Reds for Akani

Beginner   3 pots
Intermediate   15 pots
Advanced   75 pots

Coaching Top Tips and Trivia

Ash or Maple for the main shaft of your cue?

Ash absorbs shock and gives a slightly softer impact feel than Maple and is favoured by the majority of top players.

K7

TOP SPIN RED WITH FOLLOW THROUGH WHITE

Pot both red and white into the same pocket

Description

Place a red on the brown, blue and pink spot. Place the white about halfway between cushion and red ball and in a straight line.

Pot the red hitting the white top centre sending both balls into the pocket. Repeat from each position.

Why this Is a Good Exercise

1. Requires smooth cueing
2. Assists in straight cueing
3. Requires careful set up and aiming

Practice Objectives – Follow Through White

Beginner	Complete once from each position
Intermediate	Complete 3 times from each position
Advanced	3 times from each position without missing

Coaching Top Tips and Trivia

Joe Davis compiled the first officially recognized maximum break on Saturday 22 January 1955. The break was made at the home of Billiards and Snooker, the famous Thurston's Hall in Leicester Square.

K8

STRAIGHT CUEING

Placing your cue on a straight line

Description

Place 2 blocks of chalk either side of the extended baulk line and on the wooden side rail. Place the cue ball on the brown spot.

Aim to place the tip of your cue dead centre and at the bottom of the cue ball. When the cue ball is removed your tip should point at the centre of the brown spot with the cue covering the baulk line and butt in-between the blocks of chalk.

Why this Is a Good Exercise

1. Helps you to stop hitting across the cue ball
2. Ensures a consistent and correct approach to the shot
3. Encourages straight cueing on each and every shot

Practice Objectives – Straight Cueing

Beginner   30 minutes' practice
Intermediate   30 minutes' practice
Advanced   30 minutes' practice each week

Coaching Top Tips and Trivia

If your cue has a 9.5mm tip when you come to replacing it put on a 10mm tip and trim it down with a sharp knife. This is much easier than trying to place a tip on the cue that is the exact size.

K9

STRAIGHT RED STUN SHOTS

Pot and stun

Description

Straight red stun shots from each side of the table.

Set the balls as illustrated with centre reds on pink and brown spots with one ball width between the other reds.

Pot the straight reds hitting the white just below centre. The white should remain where the red was.

Aim for the right-hand side of the pocket.

Why this Is a Good Exercise

1. Improves potting skills
2. Increases control of the cue ball
3. Requires good aim and concentration

Practice Objectives – Stun Shots

Beginner	Complete once
Intermediate	Complete 2 times
Advanced	Complete 3 times without missing

Coaching Top Tips and Trivia

In 1799 John Thurston established a business based in the Strand in London making furniture and Billiard tables. In 1814 Thurston's began specializing in Billiard and Bagatelle tables.

K10

SEMI-CIRCLE CLEARANCE

Clear 12 balls

Description

Using mainly screw shots start by potting red and the yellow. Continue clearing reds and colours in sequence.

Not as easy as it looks and many good players lose control with this routine.

Why this Is a Good Exercise

1. Improves control over screw shots
2. Improves concentration
3. Requires careful thought to get in correct position for the next shot

Practice Objectives – Semi-Circle Clearance

Beginner	Clear down to the brown ball
Intermediate	Clearance
Advanced	Clearance × 3

Coaching Top Tips and Trivia

The most important piece of equipment a coach should carry in his bag? Deodorant!

K11

SCREW SHOT TRAINING

Pot red from the blue spot and screw to side cushion

Description

Place 7 reds as illustrated.

Place the white ball just off straight and aim to pot the red to middle and screw back to the side cushion.

Move the white ball just off straight for the other reds and repeat aiming to increase the power on each shot and aim to bounce the white further off the cushion.

Why this Is a Good Exercise

1. Improves potting to middle pocket
2. Increases control of the cue ball when playing screw shots
3. Increases your ability to cue smoothly and stay still on each shot

Practice Objectives – Screw Shot Training

Beginner   Spend 15 minutes practising
Intermediate   Complete the exercise
Advanced   Complete the exercise 2 times without missing

Coaching Top Tips and Trivia

The first slate bed table was introduced in 1826 and was supplied to Whites Club in London in 1832. Arguably this is the start of the modern era of billiards where the standard of play started to improve dramatically.

K12

MASTER DRILL

Score as high a score as you can

Description

Starting from any position and mainly potting into the middle pockets aim to score as high a number of pots as you can.

After each pot the red is re-spotted in its start position and each pot scores 5 points.

With practice you can score many 1000s without missing.

Why this Is a Good Exercise

1. Improves positional play
2. Requires concentration over a long period of time
3. Hit 100s or even 1000s of balls so great practice

Practice Objectives – Master Drill

Beginner   Score 50
Intermediate   Score 100
Advanced   Score 1000+

Coaching Top Tips and Trivia

It's a myth that a player can only use one cue. It is true that players never spend the practice time necessary to get used to a new cue and many cling to the notion that their cue is special.

This can be dangerous for a professional player!

K13

WORKING ON PACE

Pot and position

Description

Pot the red ball to the middle pocket and position the white ball in colour order as shown (white opposite yellow first).

Use top-spin, stun and screw shots to gain position opposite each ball in the line working from yellow down to black.

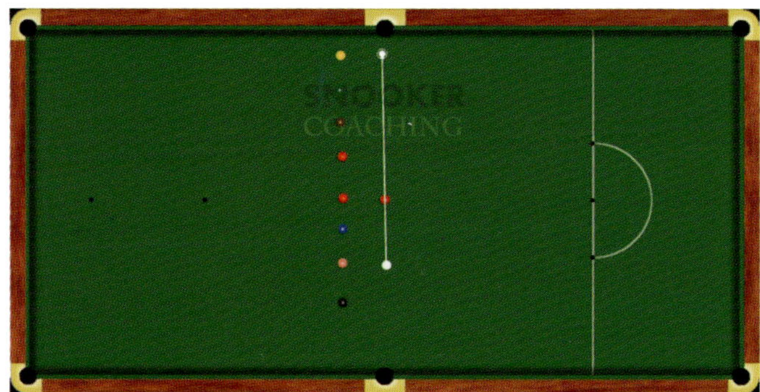

Why this Is a Good Exercise

1. Requires exacting positional play
2. Improves understanding of spins
3. Improves judgement of pace

Practice Objectives – Working on Pace

Beginner   Complete once in under 50 shots
Intermediate   Complete once in under 40 shots
Advanced   Complete once in under 20 shots

Coaching Top Tips and Trivia

Good players need to experience as many competitions as possible in order to progress. Those with the greatest drive and ability and training will have no difficulty in being ranked in the top 10 for their age group.

K14

18 BALL CLEARANCE

Clear all of the balls

Description

Starting from anywhere try to clear all of the balls in any sequence.

Play specific position on each shot and keep distance between cue ball and object ball to a minimum.

The key to this exercise is not disturbing any of the other balls whilst potting the object ball.

Why this Is a Good Exercise

1. Excellent practice
2. Improves positional play
3. Improves concentration levels

Practice Objectives – For the 18 Ball Clearance

Beginner   9 balls
Intermediate   18 ball clearance × 2
Advanced   18 ball clearance × 5

Coaching Top Tips and Trivia

Once you have found a cue you are happy and confident with please just forget it. Forget it when you are playing and let it become a part of you. Don't dwell on its beauty and don't be mesmerized by it – just play with it. Once your match or session is over then look after it and love it.

K15

BLUE POTTING ANGLES

Full, ¾, ½, ¼ ball potting on blue

Description

Here are 4 different potting angles on the blue ball (full ball ¾, ½ and ¼ ball).

The distance between balls is a ball's width.

Pot the blue ball hitting the white just above the centre from each position indicated by the red balls.

First full ball then ¾, ½ and ¼ ball pots.

Why this Is a Good Exercise

1. Learn knowledge of potting angles
2. Increases understanding of where the cue ball travels to
3. Excellent for break-building knowledge

Practice Objectives – Blue Potting Angles

Beginner	Spend 15 minutes practising
Intermediate	Spend 30 minutes practising
Advanced	Clear without missing × 3

Top Tips and Trivia

Time wasting can be a problem in the game and can, at times, be used excessively by a player to gain an advantage. The referee does have the power to disqualify a player if, after being warned, time wasting continues.

K16

SIX REDS FOR GLORY

Try to clear all of the reds without missing

Description

Nice and simple routine to warm the cue arm up.
  Place a red ball on each of the spots (6).
  Starting from anywhere aim to clear the 6 reds in one visit.
  Concentrate!

Why this Is a Good Exercise

1. Forces you into making good position on the next shot
2. Requires concentration
3. Requires a variety of shots

Practice Objectives – Six Reds for Glory

Beginner   3 reds
Intermediate   Clearance
Advanced   Clearance × 3 without missing

Coaching Top Tips and Trivia

If you want to get a rhythm into your cueing try using a metronome. Slowly but surely the background rhythm begins to penetrate your cue arm and it is not long before you are cueing with rhythm.

K17

BLACK POTTING ANGLES

Four different potting angles

Description

Here are 4 different potting angles on the black ball (full ball ¾, ½ and ¼ ball) both sides of the white ball.

The distance between balls is a ball's width.

Pot the blue ball hitting the white just above the centre from each position indicated by the red balls.

First full ball then ¾, ½ and ¼ ball pots.

Why this Is a Good Exercise

1. Excellent potting practice
2. Recognition of different potting angles
3. Essential break-building information

Practice Objectives – Black Potting Angles

Beginner   Spend 15 minutes practising
Intermediate   Spend 30 minutes practising
Advanced   All 7 pots without missing

Coaching Top Tips and Trivia

If you have a competition that's important and at a venue with which you are unfamiliar, try to get there the day before. This is not just to get used to the tables but also to reduce the stress of playing in unfamiliar surroundings.

K18

REDS AND BLUES

Try to clear all of the reds without missing

Description

Set the balls as illustrated and starting from any position try to pot as many reds and blues as you can without missing.

Why this Is a Good Exercise

1. Good for positional play
2. Requires concentration over a length of time
3. Great practice as you pot lots of balls

Practice Objectives – For Reds and Blues

Beginner	2 reds and 2 blues
Intermediate	5 reds and 5 blues
Advanced	Clearance

Coaching Top Tips and Trivia

If you have a group of juniors that you are coaching ask them to pick their favourite colour ball. Once they have done this ask them to stare at their ball for 60 seconds without laughing, talking or changing their expression. Any child who does laugh or talk is asked to sit out.

Kids love this and it really quietens them down for the snooker ahead.

K19

PINK POTTING ANGLES

Four different potting angles

Description

Here are 4 different potting angles on the pink ball (full ball ¾, ½ and ¼ ball).

The distance between balls is a ball's width.

Pot the pink ball hitting the white just above the centre from each position indicated by the red balls.

First full ball then ¾, ½ and ¼ ball pots.

Why this Is a Good Exercise

1. Excellent potting practice
2. Increases understanding of the movement of the white ball
3. Essential break-building information

Practice Objectives – Pink Potting Angles

Beginner	Spend 15 minutes practising
Intermediate	Spend 30 minutes practising
Advanced	All 4 pots without missing

Coaching Top Tips and Trivia

Spotting talent is no easy thing for a coach. You can be lead into believing that you have the greatest junior in the world in your squads who pots everything in sight but on the day of a competition the same player can't pot a thing. Practice and match play are very different things.

K20

CANNON BALL RUN

Try to pot blue and cannon into the reds

Description

Set a line of reds on the baulk line and place the blue ball on its spot.

The purpose of this exercise is to pot the blue ball and then make a cannon with each of the red balls in the line starting with the one nearest to the yellow pocket.

Once you have made the cannon remove the red ball.

Keep potting blue and working your way down the line until all of the reds have been cannoned.

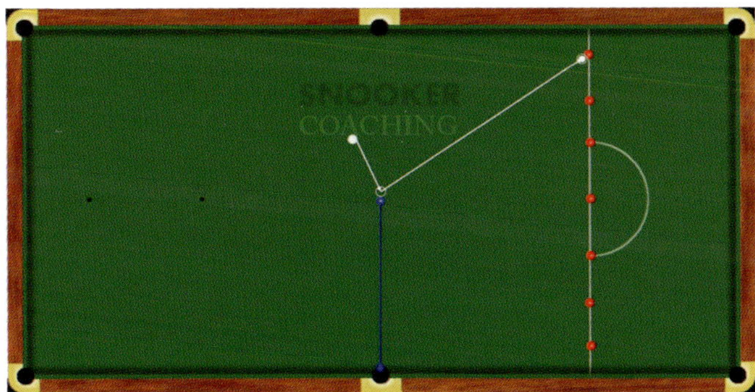

Why this Is a Good Exercise

1. Need to be proficient at stun screw and topspin shots
2. Exact positional play needed
3. Planning needed prior to taking the shot

Practice Objectives – Cannon Ball Run

Beginner   Spend 15 minutes on the exercise
Intermediate   Complete the exercise
Advanced   Complete with only 2 missed shots

Coaching Top Tips and Trivia

It may at first seem impossible and your mind may want to fight against it but practise playing with your opposite hand.

It will make some shots easier, increase your confidence and your concentration. Its also pretty frightening for your opponent!

K21

PINK POTTING ANGLES TO MIDDLE POCKET

Four different potting angles to the middle pocket

Description

There are 4 different potting angles on the pink ball (full ball ¾, ½ and ¼ ball).
   The distance between balls is a ball's width.
   Pot the pink ball hitting the white just above the centre from each position indicated by the red balls. Aim to pot left of the pocket to miss the knuckle.
   First full ball then ¾, ½ and ¼ ball pots.

Why this Is a Good Exercise

1. Increases understanding of the effect of the cloth on the object ball
2. Improves recognition of full, ¾, ½ and ¼ ball pots
3. Good potting practice

Practice Objectives – Angles to Middle Pocket

Beginner   Spend 15 minutes practising
Intermediate   Spend 30 minutes practising
Advanced   All 4 pots without missing

Coaching Top Tips and Trivia

The World Snooker Championships used to be held in a challenge format. This was changed in 1969 to the present knockout format.

K22

REDS TO BED

Try to clear the reds without missing

Description

Place 2 reds in very easy position over each pocket as illustrated in the diagram.
    Place a red on the brown, blue and black spots.
    Starting from anywhere attempt to make a clearance.

Why this Is a Good Exercise

1. Great warm-up routine
2. Builds confidence in potting
3. Some positional play needed

Practice Objectives – Reds to Bed

Beginner   6 reds
Intermediate   13 reds
Advanced   Clearance × 3 no misses

Coaching Top Tips and Trivia

Eye on the cue ball or the object ball?
    Object ball and halfway through your final backswing transfer your eyes to the object ball until the shot is played.

K23

19 POTS ON PINK

Make 19 pots on pink to various pockets

Description

Set the balls as illustrated.

Start at box 1, and pot the full ball pink into the top corner pocket, remove the red ball by the corner pocket to allow the pot.

Pot the pink into this pocket from each of the positions marked by the balls in the box.

Continue (box 2 to other top pocket, 3 to middle, 4 to other middle, 5 to middle and 6 to other middle) making 19 pots on pink.

Why this Is a Good Exercise

1. Increases knowledge of potting angles
2. Requires determination
3. Helps with break-building

Practice Objectives – 19 Pots on Pink

Beginner   Spend 30 minutes practising
Intermediate   Spend 1 hour practising
Advanced   Complete in under 30 shots

Coaching Top Tips and Trivia

The Crucible – a situation of severe trial, or in which different elements interact, leading to the creation of something new.

K24

STRAIGHT CUEING REQUIRED

Cannon at pink spot

Description

Place the cue ball on the brown spot and a red on the blue spot. Using top spin play full ball onto the red and the aim is to make a cannon by sending the red off the top cushion and back to hit the cue ball. The contact area for the cannon will be near to the pink spot.

Why this Is a Good Exercise

1. Requires straight cueing
2. Encourages laying the cue on the line of aim
3. Requires concentration and persistence

Practice Objectives – Straight Cueing

Beginner   Complete 1 out of 10
Intermediate   Complete 4 out of 10
Advanced   Complete 7 out of 10

Coaching Top Tips and Trivia

Having aimed when standing up do not take your eyes off the point on the object ball you wish to hit until your hand touches the cloth.

K25

THREE-QUARTER-BALL BLUE TO PINK

Use various spins to gain position on pink

Description

Pot the ¾ ball blue to gain position on the corresponding ball and pocket number. Once you have gained position go on to also pot the pink ball.

1. Top spin
2. Screw
3. Stun
4. Higher stun

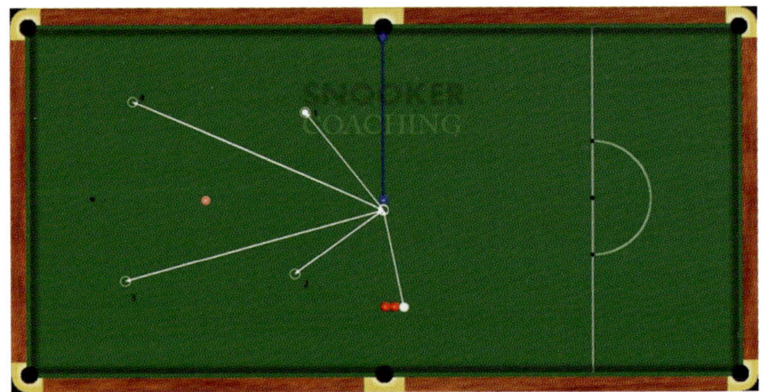

Why this Is a Good Exercise

1. Develops touch and positional play
2. Increases understanding of the various spins
3. Helps break-building

Practice Objectives – Blue to Pink

Beginner   Spend 15 minutes practising
Intermediate   Complete including pots on pink
Advanced   Complete once without missing including pink

Coaching Top Tips and Trivia

The future is going to be interesting for snooker in the UK. Many parts of the world are now playing snooker and in China there are hundreds if not thousands of professional coaches. Most coaches in the UK are part time so we need to catch up quickly or the World Championship trophy could leave these shores for many years to come.

K26

CLICK CLACK CLICK CLACK

Kiss the yellow

Description

Place a ball tight against the cushion and in a position anywhere on the table that's easy for you to reach. Place the cue ball 3 or 4 inches away from the ball on the cushion. Play little kiss shots aiming to send the cue ball back within the 3 or 4 inch distance.

Don't grip the cue too tightly!

Why this Is a Good Exercise

1. Develops a gentle touch
2. Exact striking needed
3. Develops rhythm

Practice Objectives – For Click Clack

Beginner   10 consecutive kisses
Intermediate   20 consecutive kisses
Advanced   100+ consecutive kisses

Coaching Top Tips and Trivia

In most cases it's not necessary to hit the balls hard yet in every club most players do.

Be gentle and use the minimum pace necessary for the shot and you will be surprised at how your game will improve!

K27

CONSECUTIVE REDS

Keep potting until you miss

Description

Place a red on the brown, blue and pink spots.

Place the cue ball as a ¾ ball pot on the red ball to middle pocket as indicated.

Pot the red (re-spot red) gaining position on another red. Continue like this trying to pot as many reds as you can without missing.

Remember – you must pot a different red each time!

Why this Is a Good Exercise

1. Requires exacting positional play
2. Demands pre-shot planning
3. Requires consistency

Practice Objectives – Consecutive Reds

Beginner	Pot 3 reds
Intermediate	Pot 5 reds
Advanced	Pot 25+ reds

Coaching Top Tips and Trivia

If you wish to control others you must first control yourself
- Miyamoto Musashi, *The Book Of Five Rings*

K28

SIDE SPLITTER

Split the pack off the yellow

Description

Set the balls as illustrated.

Aim to pot the yellow and do so using screw and just a trace of left-hand side, which will draw the cue ball into the pack. Quite an easy shot once mastered, but always remember the priority is the pot.

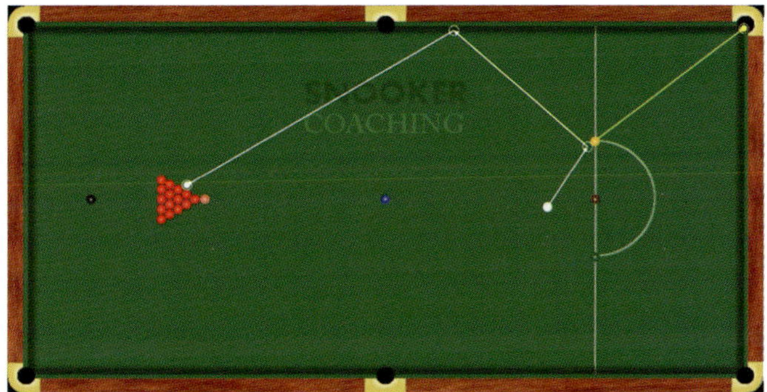

Why this Is a Good Exercise

1. Exact positional play needed
2. Develops an attacking game
3. Develops break-building skills

Practice Objectives – For Side Splitter

Beginner   1 out of 10
Intermediate   3 out of 10
Advanced   9 out of 10

Coaching Top Tips and Trivia

After you have played your stroke stay down and gain valuable knowledge about the shot you have played.

Ask yourself if you stayed still on the shot and if your tip went where you wanted it to.

Doing this encourages good habits and quick learning.

K29

BLUE BREAK CIRCLE

Stay within the circle

Description

Pot the red/blue combination keeping close control of the white ball.

Soft shots are required and you can use all of the pockets to make this a little easier.

The object is to pot reds and blues but you must stay within the circle.

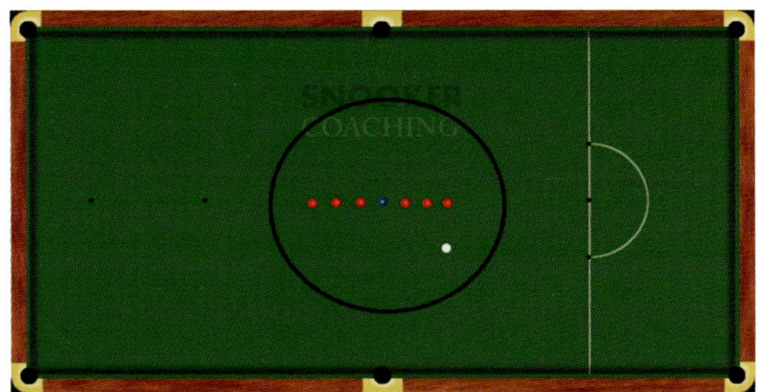

Why this Is a Good Exercise

1. Develops a soft touch when break-building
2. Tight control of the cue ball needed
3. Shot planning needed before playing your shots

Practice Objectives – Blue Break Circle

Beginner   2 reds and 1 blue
Intermediate   4 reds and 3 blues
Advanced   Clearance

Coaching Top Tips and Trivia

If you have a hard physical job and you have had a busy day avoid playing snooker if you can. Potting balls in the same way as you would normally is almost impossible after very hard physical exertion.

K30

THE AKANI SUNNY CHALLENGE

Try to clear the colours

Description

This exercise has gained worldwide popularity since I challenged Akani Sunny to complete it. He did but it takes some doing.

Set the colours as illustrated and starting from any position clear the colours in sequence.

Why this Is a Good Exercise

1. Perfect cueing required
2. Perfect positional play needed
3. Determination and concentration needed

Practice Objectives – For A.K Challenge

Beginner   10 minutes' practice
Intermediate   15 minutes' practice
Advanced   Complete just once in your career

Coaching Top Tips and Trivia

The Americans call it English and we call it side, but whatever its called it's a thing to be avoided as much as possible.

Always try to strike the centre of the ball only using side when absolutely necessary and not until you are a consistent 75+ break player.

K31

CONSECUTIVE BLACKS

Keep potting until you miss

Description

Position the white for a ¾ ball pot on the black ball to the top pocket. Pot the black and re-gain position for black again into the top pocket.

Continue potting and re-spotting for as many consecutive pots as you can without missing.

If you run out of position you can pot into other pockets if necessary but try to stay with the top pockets.

Why this Is a Good Exercise
1. Requires concentration
2. Requires pre-shot planning
3. Superb for break-building practice

Practice Objectives – Consecutive Blacks

Beginner   3 consecutive pots
Intermediate   5 consecutive pots
Advanced   10+ consecutive pots

Coaching Top Tips and Trivia

Games have got to be fun, so if a junior is working hard but not achieving what they wish just talk about the value of the hard work and endeavour. As coach or parent don't over-react, and make light of the situation.

K32

3 RED LOOP

Make as many pots as you can

Description

Place a red on the black spot, a red on the pink spot and a red in-between.
   Starting from anywhere pot a red (gaining position for the next red), re-spot the potted red and continue.
   Each red = 10 points.

Why this Is a Good Exercise

1. Improves tight positional play
2. Tests concentration
3. Excellent to improve break-building at the top end of the table

Practice Objectives – For 3 Red Loop

Beginner   30+ points
Intermediate   70+ points
Advanced   300+ points

Coaching Top Tips and Trivia

The original balls for billiards and snooker were made of wood and then ivory. Thankfully this has changed with the most popular balls being Aramith, which is a synthetic compound.

K33

BREAK BUILD IN A BOX

Get your highest break but don't go outside the box

Description

Pot the red/colour combination but you must keep the white ball inside the box.
   Try to keep on the black, pink or blue.
   Use all pockets and you can use cushions providing your final position is inside the box.
   Record your highest break before you lose position outside the box then start again!

Why this Is a Good Exercise

1. Forces you to aim for the easiest potting position on your next ball
2. Requires accuracy and concentration
3. Builds confidence and is great practice hitting lots of balls

Practice Objectives – Break Build in a Box

Beginner   15 break
Intermediate   30+ break
Advanced   Clearance

Coaching Top Tips and Trivia

When practising try to get an opponent or practice partner that you can trust to keep the score as you build a break. The chances are you will know what the score is, but if you want to focus on your break it helps to have confidence that the score is being counted.

K34

SAFETY BEHIND THE LINE

Pot the red and place the white behind the line

Description

Starting from the green spot aim to pot the red which is on the pink spot and aim to get back to the bottom cushion with the white ball in the space between bottom cushion and the line.

You can use a piece of tape for the line.

Why this Is a Good Exercise

1. Improves safety play
2. Good potting practice
3. Good for judgement of pace

Practice Objectives – Safety Behind the Line

Beginner   Complete once only
Intermediate   Complete 5 times
Advanced   Complete 10 times and 3 times in succession

Coaching Top Tips and Trivia

Every Ash cue, regardless of brand, is different due to wood being a natural material with variation in stiffness, density, grain and resonant frequency.

Maple is a stiffer material and is more consistent in feel, so many Maple cues have a similar feel.

K35

BLACK BREAK-BUILDING EXERCISE

Red and black combinations to clear the table

Description

Pot the red/black combinations, starting off with the full ball pot using top spin to gain position on the black.

Continue with red/black combinations, making the highest break that you can. Avoid ending up straight on the black.

Why this Is a Good Exercise

1. Very good for break-building knowledge around the black ball
2. Increases knowledge of which is the best shot to take
3. Requires concentration

Practice Objectives – Black Break-Building Exercise

Beginner	Pot a red/black/red
Intermediate	Pot 2 reds and 2 blacks
Advanced	Clear the table

Coaching Top Tips and Trivia

The greatest film about pool is called the 'Hustler' and starred Paul Newman as Fast Eddie Felson and Jackie Gleason as Minnesota Fats. Much of the pool action was filmed at Ames Billiard Academy in Times Square New York.

K36

AVOID THE STRAIGHT LINE POT

Pot red and black combinations but don't end up on the straight pot to black

Description

Place 2 strips of tape in a straight line with the top pockets.

Starting from any position aim to pot a red and gain position to pot black but you must not end up on the black tape (straight pot on black).

Having potted a red and black and again starting from any position repeat the combination.

Why this Is a Good Exercise

1. Helps you to avoid ending straight on the black
2. Improves positional play
3. Helps to improve break-building

Practice Objectives – Avoid the Straight Pot

Beginner   Spend 15 minutes practising
Intermediate   Complete the exercise
Advanced   Complete the exercise without missing

Coaching Top Tips and Trivia

It's not advisable to let the tip of your cue overhang, because when applying side to a ball you don't get the backing of the ferrule to ensure a solid shot.

K37

BLACK BALL BREAK-BUILDING LINE
Red/black clearance combinations

Description
Starting from position 1 aim to pot red/black combinations and try to clear the table.

Once completed repeat but this time starting from position 2.

Why this Is a Good Exercise
1. Requires tight control of the cue ball
2. Pre-shot planning needed
3. Increases break-building power

Practice Objectives – Break-Building Line
Beginner	2 reds and 1 black
Intermediate	4 reds and 3 blacks
Advanced	2 clearances from each start position

Coaching Top Tips and Trivia
Don't become a constant good loser – yes, losing is part of life and learning but being satisfied with losing means you will not work as hard as you need to in order to start winning.

K38

2 POT AND STUN SHOTS FOR STARTERS

Pot each of the reds on the side before you start your break

Description

Pot the red from the brown spot, stunning off the side cushion.

Replace the white ball on the brown spot.

Pot the long red and then pot black gaining position on a red that's in-between pink and black.

Then make the highest break you can.

Remember – unless you make the first 2 pots in succession you can't go for black and then the reds and colours.

Very tough!

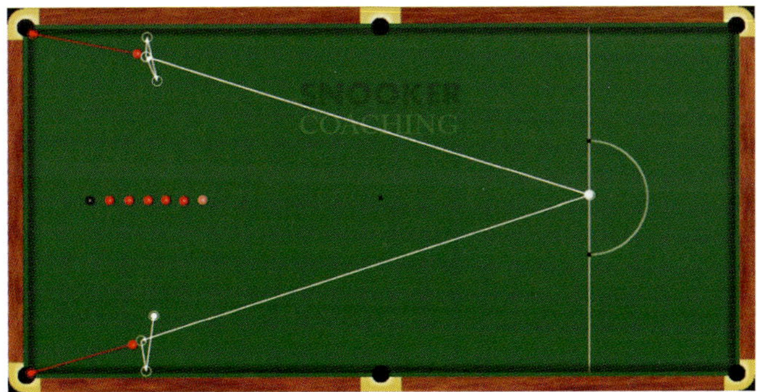

Why this Is a Good Exercise

1. Requires excellent cueing and long potting
2. Improves consistency on half chances
3. Helps break-building skills

Practice Objectives – Pot and Stun for Starters

Beginner	15 minutes practising
Intermediate	Pot the 2 reds on the side cushions
Advanced	Complete the exercise

Coaching Top Tips and Trivia

A fast cloth is a delight for a good player but a slow cloth makes for heavy going and harder for break-building. A heavier and courser cloth combined with a cold slate equals a very sluggish cloth.

Keep the snooker room warm day and night!

K39

6 REDS AND BLACKS

Red/black break-building exercise

Description

Starting from position 1 and using top-spin aim to pot red/black combinations and try to clear the table.

Once completed repeat but this time starting from position 2 and start with a stun shot.

A high level of accuracy is required for this exercise.

Why this Is a Good Exercise

1. Pinpoint accuracy is required
2. Improves break-building within a confined area
3. Requires exact pre-shot planning and almost perfect cue ball control

Practice Objectives – Reds and Blacks

Beginner	2 reds and 1 black
Intermediate	4 reds and 3 blacks
Advanced	2 clearances from each start position

Coaching Top Tips and Trivia

You may be sublimely talented with a cue action like a Rolls-Royce, but without practice, practice and more practice you will soon be a jerky shadow of your former self.

K40

RED/COLOUR SEQUENCE CLEARANCE

Pot red/colour in sequence to clear the table

Description

With a red positioned next to each colour start from any position and pot red/
yellow then repeat clearing the reds and colours in sequence.

Why this Is a Good Exercise

1. Increases skill in positional play
2. Requires pre-shot planning
3. Improves break-building and table clearance skills

Practice Objectives – For Sequence Clearance

Beginner   Spend 15 minutes practising
Intermediate   Clear down to blue ball
Advanced   2 clearances in succession

Coaching Top Tips and Trivia

There are 5 sections of slate in the bed of a full-size table and on the old tables
these can weigh over a tonne. Slate takes a long time to warm to room temperature,
so consider under-table heating to keep the table running fast.

K41

SPLIT AND BREAK

Gently split the 2 reds

Description

Starting from the position indicated, which is a ¾ ball pot on black, pot black and gently split the 2 reds as indicated.

Having done this make as big a break as you can without missing.

Why this Is a Good Exercise

1. Improves control when splitting the pack
2. Increases break-building skills
3. Requires pre-shot planning and tight cue ball control

Practice Objectives – Split And Break

Beginner   Make a 15+ break
Intermediate   Make a 24+ break
Advanced   Clear the table

Coaching Top Tips and Trivia

Are players born or made?

There is absolutely no doubt that some individuals have a natural propensity to play sport and some don't. This should not be thought of as unusual. Regardless, you still have to work incredibly hard to be good and many less natural players have gone beyond the gifted players by hard work alone.

K42

3 RED VARIANT

Pot as many reds as you can

Description

Similar but slightly easier than the one-red version of this exercise, which appeared earlier in the book.

You can start from any position to pot a red but you can't pot more than once in succession from each cluster.

Once potted the red is re-spotted in the same position.

Each pot = 10 points.

Why this Is a Good Exercise

1. Improves positional play over distance
2. Requires pre-shot planning
3. Helps break-building skills

Practice Objectives – For 3 Red Variant

Beginner   Score 30 points
Intermediate   Score 50 points
Advanced   Score 200+ points

Coaching Top Tips and Trivia

There is a good way to identify a point of contact when faced with a cut shot or tough angle. Imagine a line from the pocket to the object ball and try hitting where the line bisects the object ball. Not fool-proof but it's a good guide if you haven't practised the shot.

K43

JUDGEMENT OF PACE AND SPIN TO CANNON

Pot and cannon each of the balls in order

Description

Place the white in a position to pot the red and cannon the red on the black spot.
   Work your way round the table slightly adjusting the start position of the white in order to pot red and cannon the colours in sequence.

Why this Is a Good Exercise

1. Improves cue-ball control
2. Increases knowledge of the way the cue ball travels when hit at various heights
3. Improves break-building skills

Practice Objectives – Judgement of Pace

Beginner   Spend 15 minutes practising
Intermediate   Complete once
Advanced   Complete once but with no misses

Coaching Top Tips and Trivia

The fastest 147 or maximum break made was done so in the 1997 World Championships and was achieved by Ronnie O'Sullivan in 5 minutes and 20 seconds.

K44

TOUGH CLEARANCE

Clear the table and make a sizeable break

Description

Clear the 5 reds that are in-between pink and black spots with either pinks or blacks.

Once complete place the white behind the pink line and in a straight line with a red to bottom pocket and pot. Repeat with the other red, gaining position on yellow.

Clear the colours in sequence.

Why this Is a Good Exercise

1. Challenging and demanding, requiring concentration
2. Requires consistent play including break-building and long pots
3. Improves control over various distances

Practice Objectives – For Tough Clearance

Beginner   Spend 15 minutes practising
Intermediate   Make a 20+ break
Advanced   Clear the table – no misses

Coaching Top Tips and Trivia

To give yourself the very best chance of escaping from a snooker use the minimum pace possible.

Why?

A hard shot into a cushion narrows the angle of reflection, so you may have identified where to hit correctly but too hard and you miss the escape!

K45

BLUE AND CANNON

Pot blue and cannon reds

Description

Pot the blue ball, which is about a ¾ ball pot, and cannon into each of the reds starting with the one at the top of the line.

Work your way down the table hitting lower on each shot to make the cannon. The middle red is a stun shot and bottom red is a screw shot.

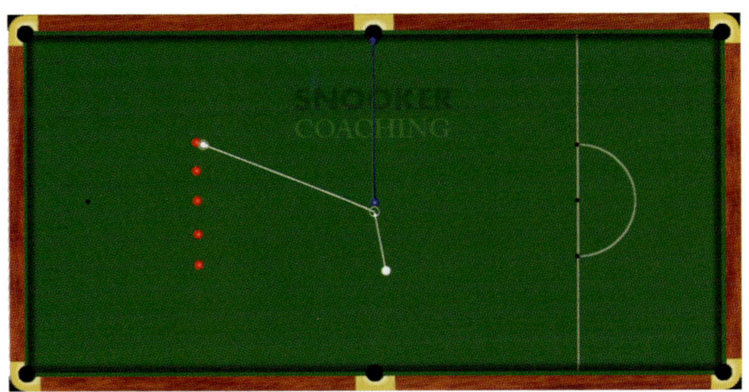

Why this Is a Good Exercise

1. Excellent potting practice on ¾ ball blue pot to middle
2. Improves control of the cue ball
3. Increases knowledge of various spins

Practice Objectives – Blue and Cannon

Beginner	Spend 15 minutes practising
Intermediate	Complete once
Advanced	Complete once without missing

Coaching Top Tips and Trivia

The greatest player of all time?

You must look to those who moved the game into a different era and in my view that's Joe Davis, Steve Davis and Stephen Hendry.

Who out of these was the greatest – it must be Joe Davis because without Joe Davis the others wouldn't be there.

K46

THE TRIPLE CANNON

Very good cueing required!

Description

This is a tough one but quite possible.

Place balls as illustrated with a red on the blue and pink spots.

Hit first red to second red, which hits top cushion and returns to strike the first red and back to the white ball for a cannon.

Very good cueing required.

Why this Is a Good Exercise

1. Perfect aiming required
2. Perfect cueing required
3. Persistence – this one may take a little time to complete

Practice Objectives – For the Triple Cannon

Beginner   Try this for 15 minutes
Intermediate   Complete once
Advanced   Complete 3 times

Coaching Top Tips and Trivia

Try to limit distance between cue ball and object ball, as potting at close range is much easier than long range when you are break-building.

K47

BLACK AND CANNON

Pot black and cannon red

Description

Pot the ¾ ball black and cannon into each of the 5 reds using various spins

Why this Is a Good Exercise

1. Superb for improving break-building skills
2. Increases control and understanding of various spins
3. Requires pre-shot planning

Practice Objectives – Black and Cannon

Beginner   Spend 15 minutes practising
Intermediate   Complete once
Advanced   Complete once without missing

Coaching Top Tips and Trivia

The Crucible Theatre is regarded as the home for the World Championships but the seating capacity is only 980 people and for the game to grow so must the venue.

K48

SAFETY BEHIND THE LINE

Play a safety shot placing the white ball behind the line

Description

Place the balls as illustrated with a red in the D and a line of colours either side of the black that is on its spot.

Play a safety shot aiming to come off 4 cushions placing the white ball behind the line of colours and snookering on the red ball.

Why this Is a Good Exercise

1. Improves safety play over distance
2. Helps with judgement of pace
3. Increases tactical awareness

Practice Objectives – Safety Behind the Line

Beginner   Spend 15 minutes practising
Intermediate   Complete once
Advanced   Complete 5 times

Coaching Top Tips and Trivia

A cue ball will transfer momentum to another ball, confirming Newton's first law that an object will remain at rest or in motion until acted upon by another.

K49

BREAK-BUILDING ON BLUE

Pot as many reds and blues as you can

Description

Starting from any position try to pot as many reds and blues as you can.

Not as easy as it first appears due to the comparatively large distance between red and blue.

You can use all of the pockets and cushions for this exercise.

Why this Is a Good Exercise

1. Builds break-building skills
2. Requires very good control of the cue ball
3. Concentration and pre-shot planning needed

Practice Objectives – Break-Building on Blue

Beginner   2 reds and 1 blue
Intermediate   4 reds and 3 blues
Advanced   2 full clearances with no miss

Coaching Top Tips and Trivia

If you are the parent of a junior receiving coaching try to leave your child in the capable hands of the coach rather than be sat over your child. You will find your child becomes more outgoing and mixes better and in the end is likely to enjoy the process and be more successful.

K50

COLOURS AND REDS

Start by potting the colours in sequence

Description

Place the balls as illustrated with a line of reds across the middle of the table and the colours on the outer edge as shown.

Start by clearing the colours in sequence and having potted the final colour (black) pot all of the reds into any pocket.

Why this Is a Good Exercise

1. Requires accurate positional play
2. Improves concentration over an extended period of potting
3. Pre-shot planning required

Practice Objectives – For the Colours and Reds

Beginner   Spend 15 minutes practising
Intermediate   Clear the colours
Advanced   Clear the colours and the reds

Coaching Top Tips and Trivia

When hitting with spin, the ball that is struck does gain some spin but so little that it makes virtually no difference at all. It is more affected by the cue ball's direction.

K51

RED AND COLOUR BREAK-BUILDING EXERCISE

Pot each red then clear yellow, green and brown

Description

Starting from position 1 pot a red to the middle pocket using top spin and gaining position on the yellow ball. Pot yellow, green and brown. Repeat with the other 2 reds, slightly adjusting the start position.

Once complete start from position 2 but use a screw shot to gain position on yellow. Again pot yellow, green and brown.

Repeat with the other 2 reds, slightly adjusting the start position.

Why this Is a Good Exercise

1. Requires tight positional play over distance
2. Requires concentration
3. Excellent potting practice, particularly on the colours

Practice Objectives – Break-Building Exercise

Beginner   Spend 30 minutes practising
Intermediate   Spend 45 minutes practising
Advanced   Complete 3 times

Coaching Top Tips and Trivia

The collective noun for a group of snooker players is – a pack of snooker players. An equally appropriate description could be a pyramid of snooker players.

K52

COLOUR CANNON LINE

Off 2 cushions to cannon

Description

Starting from any position behind the baulk line aim to come off side and top cushions to cannon the colours in sequence.

Aim to cannon each colour down to black without missing. Once you cannon a colour remove it from the table.

Once completed, take the white back into the D and split the reds. Aim to clear the reds into any pocket without missing.

Why this Is a Good Exercise

1. Very challenging and requiring knowledge of angles off cushions
2. Improves safety play
3. Improves snooker escapes

Practice Objectives – Colour Cannon Line

Beginner	Aim to cannon each colour
Intermediate	Cannon each colour and pot 2 reds
Advanced	Cannon each colour, no misses and pot 10+ reds

Coaching Top Tips and Trivia

Every action has an equal and opposite reaction according to our friend Newton, explaining why the cue ball bounces off the cushion when it hits it.

K53

JUDGEMENT DAY

Pot red and go in-between the colours

Description

Pot the ½ ball red using a soft top spin to bounce the white off the top cushion and between the yellow and green balls.

Continue to work through the colours applying the correct spin.

More power for the middle balls and less power required for black and pink balls.

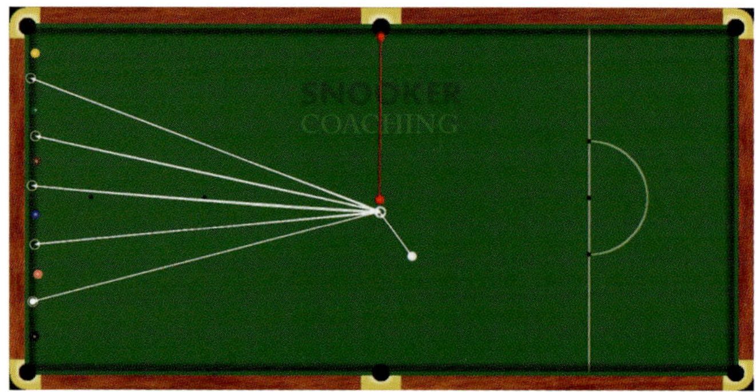

Why this Is a Good Exercise

1. Increases knowledge of the trajectory of the cue ball
2. Good ½ ball potting practice
3. Increases knowledge of top-spin, stun and screw shots

Practice Objectives – Judgement Day

Beginner   Complete in under 15 shots
Intermediate   Complete in under 12 shots
Advanced   Complete in under 7 shots

Coaching Top Tips and Trivia

When you are playing position on a colour try to avoid landing straight. Try to give yourself an angle that makes position on your next shot much easier.

Practice this; it's important!

K54

KILLER COLOUR CLEARANCE

Try to clear the table (if you can)

Description

This is an advanced routine and a very tough one for any player.

Each colour has 3 reds next to it apart from black. Starting with the reds next to yellow, pot red/yellow (re-spot yellow) and repeat with the other 2 reds.

Once 3 reds and 3 yellows have been potted repeat with the other reds and colours in sequence, finishing by potting black.

Why this Is a Good Exercise

1. Requires advanced break-building skills
2. Really sharpens up your positional play
3. Shows where you are up to as a player

Practice Objectives – For Killer Colour Clearance

Beginner	See how far you get
Intermediate	Clear to green
Advanced	Clear the table once only

Coaching Top Tips and Trivia

The first World Professional Snooker Championships were held in 1927 and the winner was of course the great Joe Davis, who went on to win the title 15 times.

K55

POT AND STUN

Pot red into corner using a stun shot

Description

Pot the full-ball reds into the top left and top right corner pockets using a stun shot.

   Start with the reds halfway between the blue and the baulk line, then move further away to the blue spot as you improve.

   The further the distance to the red, the more difficult the shot.

Why this Is a Good Exercise

1. Perfectly straight cueing is required
2. Stillness on each of the shots is needed
3. A consistent approach to each shot is needed

Practice Objectives – Pot and Stun

Beginner   2 out of 10
Intermediate   5 out of 10
Advanced   9 out of 10

Coaching Top Tips and Trivia

How good was Alex Higgins?

   Well I can speak from experience here as Alex came to a club in my area in the late 1970s. At the time there were many very good players but none of them could get near Higgins who had 2 centuries plus a break over 50 in every frame he played – he was good – very good!

K56

THE PINK CROSS

Try to clear all of the reds without missing

Description

Place reds and pink as illustrated in the diagram.

Aim to pot the 12 reds with 12 pinks into any pocket. This is a tough clearance for anybody, so keep practising this one and your game and control of the cue ball will improve.

You can start this exercise from any position that you prefer.

Why this Is a Good Exercise

1. Exact positional play is needed
2. Excellent control of the cue ball
3. Concentration and persistence

Practice Objectives – For the Pink Cross

Beginner   2 reds and 1 pink
Intermediate   4 reds and 4 pinks
Advanced   Clearance

Coaching Top Tips and Trivia

Your aim may be perfect and your cue action perfect, but if you move on the shot you will never be a great player.

Nothing moves apart from the cue arm and it is something you must practise on every shot for all of the time that you play snooker.

K57

FULL-BALL POT ON RED

Pot red, stop white dead

Description

This is a full-ball pot on red starting with the white on the yellow spot.

Pot the red into the top pocket with a powerful stun shot to stop the white on impact.

Lengthen the cue to generate the power and try the shot from both sides of the table.

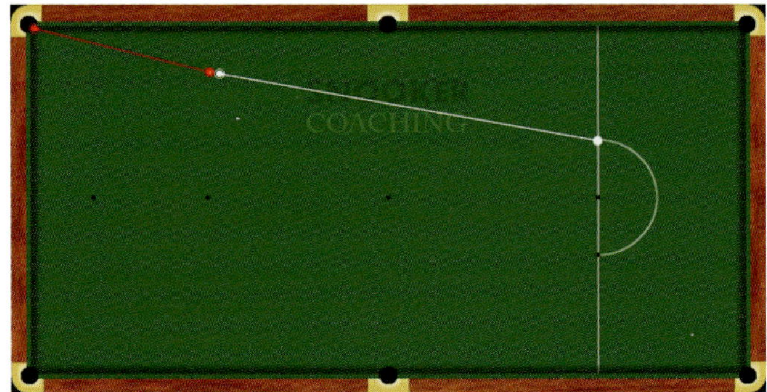

Why this Is a Good Exercise

1. Requires perfectly straight cueing
2. Requires perfect stillness on the shot
3. Improves the use of stun shots over distance

Practice Objectives – Pot on Red

Beginner	Spend 15 minutes practising
Intermediate	Complete once from both sides of the table
Advanced	Complete twice in succession from each side

Coaching Top Tips and Trivia

The first recognized snooker century break was made in 1922 and was a 113 made by a Mr Stanbury.

The first player to record 1000 centuries was Horace Lindrum and the first century by a woman was made by Alison Fisher in 1987.

K58

SIMPLE LINE

Clear all of the balls

Description

Nice and easy but still a challenge even for the best players.

Place a full line of balls across the table and in any order. Starting from any position aim to clear the line.

Advanced players can aim to clear multiple times without missing.

Why this Is a Good Exercise

1. Improves shot planning
2. Concentration needed over lengthy periods of potting
3. Good for break-building

Practice Objectives – For the Simple Line

Beginner	Clear 10 balls
Intermediate	Clear 1 full line of balls
Advanced	Clear 3 times in succession

Coaching Top Tips and Trivia

Try practising to classical music. Something about having classical music playing in a snooker club creates a perfect atmosphere to relax and concentrate.

Give it a try!

K59

HALF-BALL RED – FIXED WHITE

Pot red and send white into baulk

Description

The ½ ball red is in line with the pink spot and the white, which is placed on the yellow spot.

Pot the red with top spin to get the white back behind the baulk line near to the cushion.

Repeat the same shot but from the left side of the table.

Why this Is a Good Exercise

1. Improves long potting
2. Increases cue ball control over distance
3. Improves safety play

Practice Objectives – Fixed White

Beginner   Spend 15 minutes practising this shot
Intermediate   Complete each side once
Advanced   Complete 3 times in succession

Coaching Top Tips and Trivia

The first televised game of snooker was shown in 1937 and featured Horace Lindrum v Willie Smith.

K60

TRIANGLE OF CONFUSION

Split the reds and pot them plus the colours

Description

This one turned out to be something of an online sensation!
Set the colours inside the triangle as illustrated.
Pot red to middle, splitting the pack.
First pot all the reds – no miss and then pot the colours in sequence.
Can it be done?
YES.

Why this Is a Good Exercise

1. Excellent practice at splitting the pack
2. Significantly improves break-building skills
3. Requires concentration and determination

Practice Objectives – Triangle of Confusion

Beginner	Try just to split the pack once
Intermediate	Split the pack and clear 3 reds
Advanced	Complete just once

Coaching Top Tips and Trivia

There is absolutely no doubt at all about whom the greatest billiard player of all time is. Of course it is Walter Lindrum who took the game to new heights and whose highest break was 4137.

K61

ADVANCED LONG-POTTING ANGLES

Pot the reds and get the white ball back into baulk

Description

In this exercise the red always remains in the same position, which is half-way in from the pink spot to the cushion.

There are 3 different potting angles (¾, ½ and ¼ ball pots).

Aim from position 1 to pot the red with top spin to get the white back behind the baulk line and near the cushion.

Repeat from the other positions and each side of the table.

Why this Is a Good Exercise

1. Good practice for ¾, ½ and ¼ ball recognition
2. Increases understanding of the use of top spin
3. Improves cue ball control

Practice Objectives – Long Potting Angles

Beginner   Spend 15 minutes practising
Intermediate   Complete once
Advanced   Complete 3 times

Coaching Top Tips and Trivia

It was in 1835 that the first natural rubber cushions were introduced and these replaced cushions that were previously stuffed with layers of felt padding.

K62

EASY CLEARANCE TO GET THE SESSION STARTED

Good little warm-up routine to get the cue arm moving

Description

Start off clearing the reds in between the pink and black, only potting the pink or black balls.

Once you have done that, on the final pot gain position on the red next to blue – pot the red and blue gaining position on the red next to yellow. Pot red yellow then red green and red brown.

Why this Is a Good Exercise

1. Great warm-up routine at the start of a session
2. Improves accurate positional play
3. Easy, so good for building confidence

Practice Objectives – For Easy Clearance

Beginner	Spend 15 minutes practising
Intermediate	Make a 20+ break
Advanced	Clear the table once

Coaching Top Tips and Trivia

Described by Joe Davis as the great Mecca, the Holy of Holies, of the game was Thurstons in Leicester Square, London. Built in 1901 and reserved strictly for top class tournaments, sadly shattered in 1940 by a German Land mine. It was what Lords is to cricket and Wimbledon to tennis.

K63

RED TO BLACK POSITIONAL PLAY

Pot reds and gain position to pot black

Description

Set up the 3 reds as shown giving ¾, full and ¾ ball left side pots.

The first pot is the red nearest the side cushion, which you pot using top spin. The next pot is full ball using bottom spin to stop the white ball. The final shot is top spin again to gain position on black.

Repeat on both sides of the table and pot the black if you can.

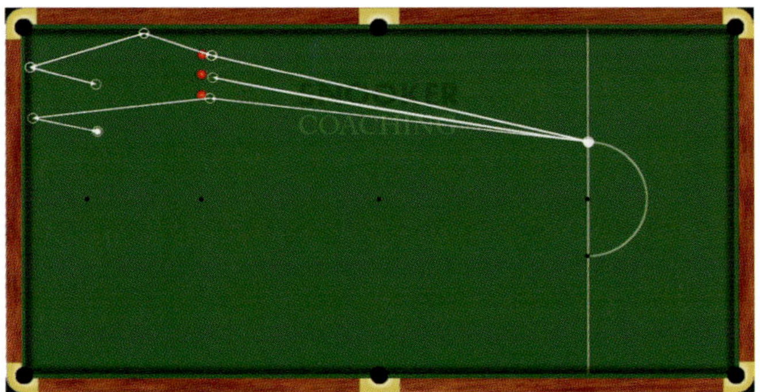

Why this Is a Good Exercise

1. Requires straight cueing and stillness on the shot
2. Improves potting and positional play
3. Requires concentration

Practice Objectives – Black Positional Play

Beginner   Spend 15 minutes practising
Intermediate   Complete from one side only
Advanced   Complete from both sides

Coaching Top Tips and Trivia

A cueist is a person skilled in cue sports. A billiard player also can be known as a billiardist or cueman.

K64

TOUGH BREAK

Split the pack and make a break

Description

This one is pretty tough I am afraid, however it's also realistic as often the reds don't fall in pretty patterns and you still have to make the most of them.

Starting from any position split the pack and then aim to make as big a break as you can with red/black combinations.

Why this Is a Good Exercise

1. Requires very accurate positional play
2. Takes you out of the comfort zone of regular patterns
3. Need perseverance and concentration

Practice Objectives – For Tough Break

Beginner   Spend 15 minutes practising this one
Intermediate   Make a 17+ break
Advanced   Make a 50+ break

Coaching Top Tips and Trivia

Alec Brown playing against Tom Newman at snooker having been left with the cue ball tightly tucked in the middle of the reds, almost impossible to use a rest or spider, produced from his waistcoat pocket a pencil with a tip on it and moved the white slightly. It was deemed to be a foul shot by the referee as it was not a cue!

K65

THE CLOCK ROUTINE

Stay within the circle

Description

Place the white just off centre of the chosen red and pot with a soft screw shot to gain position on the next red for a similar shot.

   Pot all the reds using all the pockets, but the white must remain within the circle of reds.

Why this Is a Good Exercise

1.   Develops touch and control
2.   Build confidence break-building in a confined area
3.   Requires concentration

Practice Objectives – The Clock Routine

Beginner   3 reds
Intermediate   8 reds
Advanced   12 reds

Coaching Top Tips and Trivia

The Anchor Cannon is a billiards position in which the object balls are jammed inside the jaws of a pocket in such a way that they are not frozen to one another. In days gone by huge scores were amassed by keeping the balls in this position and scoring hundreds if not thousands of cannons.

K66

PERFECT POSITIONAL PLAY

A very tough colour clearance

Description

Pretty tough but it has been done many times.

Set the colours as illustrated and also the reds, which are blocking the majority of the potting positions on the colours.

Start from about where the white ball is shown and try to clear the colours in sequence. Once complete then clear the reds.

Pinpoint accuracy required!

Why this Is a Good Exercise

1. Requires excellent cue ball control
2. Pinpoint accuracy and judgement of pace needed
3. A high level of skill required and persistence

Practice Objectives – Perfect Positional Play

Beginner   2 colours
Intermediate   3 colours
Advanced   Clearance

Coaching Top Tips and Trivia

Although published many years ago Joe Davis books, particularly *Complete Snooker*, stand out as the best instructional information ever written about snooker. Parts are now dated, but even so much of Joe's information is still relevant to this day.

K67

BLACK BREAK-BUILDING EXERCISE

Start with a ¾ ball pot on red

Description

Pot the red/black combinations in a clockwise/anticlockwise order.

A good angle on the black is required to gain position on the next red.

Use all pockets and cushions and there are 2 different starting points each side of the black.

Why this Is a Good Exercise

1. Accurate positional play needed
2. Pre-shot planning required
3. Concentration needed

Practice Objectives – Break-Building Exercise

Beginner	Pot 2 reds and 1 black
Intermediate	Pot 3 reds and 2 blacks
Advanced	Clear 2 times in succession – no miss!

Coaching Top Tips and Trivia

Feeling nervous? A few minutes of deep breathing will settle your nerves and energize you for the match ahead.

K68

STAR PERFORMER

Split the pack and pot all of the balls

Description

Starting from anywhere inside the D split the pack of balls and aim to pot all of the reds.

Once you pot the reds aim to clear the colours in sequence.

Why this Is a Good Exercise

1. It is good fun and a challenge
2. Requires good positional play
3. Improves break-building skills

Practice Objectives – For Star Performer

Beginner   Pot 3 reds in succession
Intermediate   Clear 6+ reds
Advanced   Clear all the reds and colours in sequence

Coaching Top Tips and Trivia

No snooker library is complete without a copy of Joe Davis's book called *The Breaks Came My Way*.

A truly fascinating read about a billiards and snooker genius.

K69

PINK BREAK-BUILDING LINE

Hold the line!

Description

Pot the red/pink combination keeping the white under tight control and not far away from the line.

Soft controlled shots are required plus some planning before you take the shot. You can use all the pockets and cushions if needed.

Why this Is a Good Exercise

1. Pre-shot planning needed
2. Develops touch and control
3. Excellent for break-building in a tight area

Practice Objectives – Pink Break-Building Line

Beginner   2 reds and 1 pink
Intermediate   3 reds and 2 pinks
Advanced   Clearance

Coaching Top Tips and Trivia

What is a stun shot?

If the cue ball and object ball are in a perfect straight line a stun shot means stopping the cue ball dead on impact. If the shot is at an angle the stun shot widens the angle at which the cue ball leaves the object ball.

K70

SPLIT THE CIRCLE

Pot yellow to middle and break the circle

Description

Pot the yellow ball to the middle pocket and split the circle with the cue ball.
Continue potting the colours in sequence then pot all of the reds.
   Be careful not to use too much pace splitting the balls.
   Some luck involved, but it's not as hard as it looks.

Why this Is a Good Exercise

1. Good practice splitting the pack
2. Accurate positional play needed
3. Requires pre-shot planning and concentration

Practice Objectives – Split the Circle

Beginner   Split the pack
Intermediate   Split the pack plus clear to blue
Advanced   Split and complete clearance

Coaching Top Tips and Trivia

At some point in the future someone in the film industry is going to write a script
about the rivalry between Joe Davis and Walter Lindrum. Now an almost forgotten
story, but what a story about possibly the two greatest players to pick up a cue,
meeting at the height of their genius.

K71

HALF-BALL COLOUR CANNONS

Half–ball and cannon

Description

Pot the ½ ball red off the black spot to cannon each of the 6 colours using various spins.
    Yellow to brown use stun shots
    Blue use top spin
    Pink to black use running LH side
    Try from both sides of the table

Why this Is a Good Exercise

1. Helps you recognize a ½ ball pot
2. Increases knowledge of when to use various spins
3. Develops judgement of pace

Practice Objectives – Colour Cannons

Beginner	Complete in under 60 shots
Intermediate	Complete in under 40 shots
Advanced	Complete in under 10 shots

Coaching Top Tips and Trivia

When you are break-building try your best to keep the cue ball well away from the cushions (unless the situation demands this) and avoid bridging over balls as it is difficult and often requires hitting down on the shot and accidentally imparting side spin on the cue ball.

K72

MINI MACHINE-GUN SHOT

Yellow and blue before the white

Description

Hit the white at a slow pace for the top pocket and then hit blue and yellow for the same pocket.

You must pot all three balls but the white ball must go in last.

Why this Is a Good Exercise

1. Frees up your cueing and natural ability
2. Builds up confidence
3. Requires good coordination

Practice Objectives – Mini Machine-Gun Shot

Beginner   Complete once
Intermediate   Complete twice
Advanced   Complete 3 times in succession

Coaching Top Tips and Trivia

Can a player who has not been coached and who doesn't have a good technique win a World Championship in the future?

No or at best highly unlikely – the game has changed and has entered a new era where coaching plays a central part as with other sports like football and tennis.

K73

HALF-BALL CANNON TO REDS

Pot black and cannon each bunch of reds

Description

Pot the half-ball black from the start position indicated and cannon into each bunch of reds using various spins (top-spin, stun, running side centre left).

For running side it's a balance between how much you compensate on the potting angle and how much left spin you put on.

Why this Is a Good Exercise

1. Great potting practice
2. Control of the cue ball
3. Increases understanding of spins

Practice Objectives – Cannon to Reds

Beginner   Spend 20 minutes practising
Intermediate   Complete within 20 shots
Advanced   Complete within 6 shots

Coaching Top Tips and Trivia

Fitness is important if you want to feel fit, healthy and alert for the duration of a match. You don't need to be superman, just sensibly fit, and for this you can get advice from your local gym.

K74

COLOUR TRIANGLE SPLIT AND CLEAR

Split the pack and clear in sequence

Description

From about the position indicated pot the red ball into the yellow pocket coming off the side cushion to split the pack.

Clear the colours in sequence.

Some luck required with the split, but if you keep pace to a minimum it is quite possible.

Why this Is a Good Exercise

1. Very good practice splitting the pack off the yellow-ball position
2. Good judgement of angle and pace required
3. Improves break-building and positional play

Practice Objectives – Triangle Split

Beginner	Split the pack only
Intermediate	Split the pack and clear to brown
Advanced	Complete the exercise

Coaching Top Tips and Trivia

Try a game of Snooker Plus if you wish to make a high break. First introduced by Joe Davis in 1959, the game has two extra colours, an orange and a purple ball. The orange is worth 8 points and is placed in-between pink and blue, and purple worth 10 points is placed in-between blue and brown. The game is played in the same way as snooker.

K75

EASY POSITION BIGGEST BREAK OPPORTUNITY

Starting from any position make the biggest break that you can

Description

Starting from any position with the cue ball try to make as big a break as you possibly can without missing.

For the above-average player start at the reds at the baulk end of the table and then work your way down the table.

Why this Is a Good Exercise

1. Increases a player's confidence in being able to make sizeable breaks
2. Requires concentration over an extended period of time
3. Improves cue ball control

Practice Objectives – Break Opportunity

Beginner   Make a 15+ break
Intermediate   Make a 30+ break
Advanced   Make a 70+ break

Coaching Top Tips and Trivia

To develop as a player in this modern age of snooker you need to start the game very young. Juniors of 7 years of age are beginning to play and receive coaching. If you only started playing the game at 18 I am afraid that the possibility of becoming World Champion is very remote indeed.

K76

THE LINE

Make as big a break as you can

Description

This is a practice routine that goes back almost as far as the invention of the game itself.

Start from any position potting red and colour and try to clear the table.

Why this Is a Good Exercise

1. A great way to get in practice
2. Improves positional play
3. A good measure of your improvement

Practice Objectives – For The Line

Beginner   20 break
Intermediate   50 break
Advanced   100+ break

Coaching Top Tips and Trivia

Learn how to put a tip on your cue – you don't need to be an expert in DIY.

Virtually anybody can put a tip on their cue – it's not rocket science!

Take a look on YouTube for tutorials on this.

K77

USING THE REST EFFECTIVELY

Pot reds into all 4 corner pockets

Description

From each of the positions indicated by the X mark use the rest to pot straight reds into all 4 corner pockets.

Use top spin, stun and screw shots.

Remember to stand square to the shot and keep the same bridge distance as with the hand.

Why this Is a Good Exercise

1. Improves competency with the rest
2. Improves technique
3. Assists with break-building

Practice Objectives – Using the Rest

Beginner   Spend 15 minutes practising
Intermediate   Complete 4 of each spin into each pocket
Advanced   Complete 8 of each spin into each pocket

Coaching Top Tips and Trivia

In American pool it's a draw shot and in snooker a screw shot. Developments in cloth and ball technology mean that this once mysterious shot is now played by almost every player.

K78

POT AND SCREW TO LINE

Pot yellow and screw to the line

Description

Pot the yellow into the middle pocket and screw off side and top cushion for contact on one of the reds in the line.

If this is easy then remove each of the reds you make contact with and try to clear the line.

Why this Is a Good Exercise

1. Improves control of the screw shot
2. Requires excellent cueing and ball control
3. Improves concentration

Practice Objectives – Pot and Screw

Beginner   Pot yellow 3 times
Intermediate   Pot yellow and contact red once
Advanced   Pot yellow and contact each red in the line

Coaching Top Tips and Trivia

Traditionally known as the Maximum, which is 147 points and is achieved by potting all reds with blacks and then the colours. The highest possible break is known as the Super Maximum and is achieved when your opponent leaves a free ball with the black being potted as the additional colour plus a normal maximum break.

K79

BREAK-BUILDING 3-POSITION START

Clear the table if you can

Description

There are 3 different start positions for this exercise.
   Pot the red/colour combinations keeping the white ball within the box indicated.
   Try your best to keep on the black, pink or blue balls.
   Make the highest break that you can.

Why this Is a Good Exercise

1. Improves very tight cue ball control
2. Improves break-building capability
3. Improves pre-shot planning

Practice Objectives – 3 Position Start

Beginner	Spend 15 minutes practising this exercise
Intermediate	At least a 20+ break from each start position
Advanced	At least a 40+ break from each start position

Coaching Top Tips and Trivia

God Bless You is a mnemonic phrase used by those new to the game of snooker in order to remember the placement of the baulk colours. Green, Brown, Yellow – God Bless You!

K80

STAY BEHIND THE LINE

Make a break but your cue ball must not pass beyond the black line

Description

This is a bit tricky so think about it carefully.

There is a potential 56 break on here by potting red/black combinations, but at no point must your white ball pass over the black line.

You can pot into any pocket.

Why this Is a Good Exercise

1. Very tight control required
2. Careful pre-shot planning needed
3. Improves break-building skills

Practice Objectives – Stay Behind the Line

Beginner   Make a break of 9+
Intermediate   Make a break of 17+
Advanced   Complete a clearance

Coaching Top Tips and Trivia

A full-size table measures 11ft 8½ inches × 5ft 10 inches and is commonly referred to as 12 × 6ft.

K81

BREAK-BUILDING EXERCISE

Pot red and gain position on brown

Description

There are 2 start positions. Number 1 is full ball, which requires a screw shot to gain position on brown.

Number 2 is a ½ to ¾ ball pot requiring soft top spin to retain position on brown.

Aim to pot brown then clear the colours.

Why this Is a Good Exercise

1. Improves control at the bottom end of the table
2. Increases the understanding of movement of the cue ball
3. Improves break-building skills

Practice Objectives – Break-Building Exercise

Beginner	Spend 15 minutes practising
Intermediate	Complete both pots on reds/browns once
Advanced	Clear the table twice from both positions

Coaching Top Tips and Trivia

A splice is the joining of various woods with glue. The butts of decorative cues are formed by splicing two or more woods together, often using a veneer.

K82

POT AND CANNON OFF GREEN SPOT

Find the gap and make the cannon

Description

Place the balls as illustrated.

Make a pot on the red that's on the green spot, sending the white ball off the side cushion through the gap between the two lines of reds, off the opposite side cushion to make a cannon on the first red.

Once complete repeat the exercise on the second and third reds.

Why this Is a Good Exercise

1. Requires good control of the cue ball over distance
2. Excellent practice to gain position for black when playing off the green ball
3. Very good potting practice

Practice Objectives – Pot and Cannon

Beginner	Pot and find the gap at least once
Intermediate	Pot and make the first cannon
Advanced	Complete the exercise twice

Coaching Top Tips and Trivia

Hard to get an exact figure but it is estimated that there are now over 70 million people playing snooker in China alone.

K83

THREE-QUARTER-BALL POT AND RETURN

Pot the red and return to baulk

Description

The ¾ ball red is achieved by placing the white on the yellow spot and setting up a red as a full-ball pot to the corner pocket. Next place a red just above this ball and this is the ¾ ball pot that you will attempt.

Pot the red with top spin to get the white back around the blue spot or beyond if you possess the cueing and power.

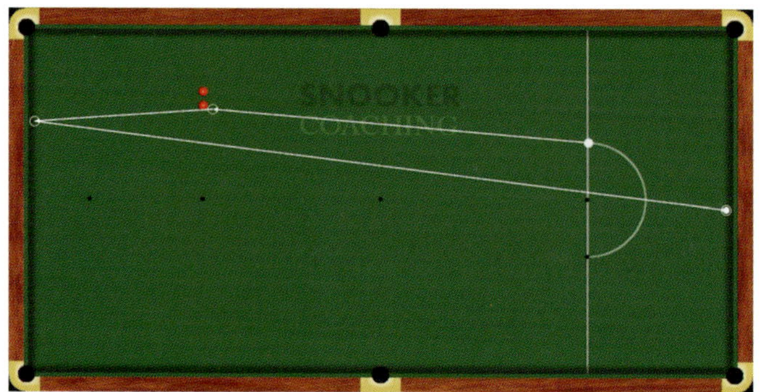

Why this Is a Good Exercise

1. Good potting practice over distance
2. Requires good aim and cueing
3. Improves understanding of top spin over distance

Practice Objectives – Pot and Return

Beginner   Practise for 15 minutes
Intermediate   Complete from both sides once only
Advanced   Complete both sides twice in succession

Coaching Top Tips and Trivia

Cue chalk is not made of chalk (calcium carbonate), but is made with a mixture of gritty silica and mixed with a colourant and suspended in a fixative. This is then baked into a cube shape.

K84

COLOUR CLEARANCE AVOIDING THE OBSTACLES

Clear the colours in sequence

Description

Start from anywhere inside the D and aim to clear the colours in sequence. After potting the pink ball gain position on the red next to the black, which you pot and then pot black.

To make it really challenging advance players can then try to clear all of the remaining reds.

At no point in the clearance must the cue ball touch any of the reds in the line or either of the triangles.

Why this Is a Good Exercise

1. Tight positional play needed
2. Pre-shot planning required
3. High level of concentration and focus needed

Practice Objectives – Avoid Obstacles

Beginner	Clear down to green
Intermediate	Clear down to pink
Advanced	Complete clearance including reds

Coaching Top Tips and Trivia

It can be argued that the TV programme *Pot Black* played a very large part in the huge growth of the game of snooker in the 1970s and 1980s. The first programme was in 1969 and the game has never looked back since then. The great John Spencer was the first winner of *Pot Black*.

K85

UP AND DOWN THE SPOTS WITH MARKER BALLS

Try to avoid the reds and go back into baulk

Description

Place a chalk on the cushion in line with the black spot as illustrated.

Aim at the chalk and try to send the white ball over the spots and back into baulk whilst avoiding contact with the reds which are just over a ball width apart.

Why this Is a Good Exercise

1. Requires good aiming
2. Improves straight cueing
3. Improves judgement of pace

Practice Objectives – Over the Spots

Beginner   3 out of 10
Intermediate   8 out of 10
Advanced   10 out of 10

Coaching Top Tips and Trivia

The first known indoor billiard table belonged to King Louis XI of France and dates back to the 15th century.

K86

POT AND BANANA SHOT TO GREEN POCKET

Have a bit of fun with this one

Description

As well as training hard sometimes you need to just have a bit of fun!
   Place the black on its spot and the white ball approximately where illustrated.
   Pot black using lots of top spin and aim to arc the white ball into the top pocket.

Why this Is a Good Exercise

1. Increases cue power control over distance
2. Good potting practice when playing at pace
3. It is fun!

Practice Objectives – Banana Shot

Beginner   Pot black 3 times
Intermediate   Spend 15 minutes trying this exercise
Advanced   Complete 3 times

Coaching Top Tips and Trivia

The vast majority of snooker players will play on a regular basis but will never make a break above 70 in their lives.
   It looks easy on television but still remains one of the hardest games to play.

K87

BLUE/RED LOOP

Pot as many reds and blues as you can

Description

Here is a great challenge and one that will help your break-building.

Set the balls as illustrated with a slight angle on the red to gain position on blue.

Pot red and re-spot – gain position on blue, which you pot and again gain position on red.

Continue like this and make as many continuous loops of red/blues as you can.

Why this Is a Good Exercise

1. Improves break-building skills
2. Pre-shot planning needed
3. Improves positional play and cue ball control

Practice Objectives – Blue/Red Loop

Beginner	2 loops
Intermediate	4 loops
Advanced	10+ loops

Coaching Top Tips and Trivia

Use visualisation as a method to build your confidence before playing a match. It can have a remarkable impact on your game.

K88

POT SCREW POT

Power up for this exercise

Description

Enjoy really hitting through this shot!

Place balls as illustrated and start by playing a powerful screw shot to pot firstly the pink ball and then arc the white ball to the green pocket and pot the yellow ball – all in the same shot.

Repeat with black and the blue ball.

Don't hold back!

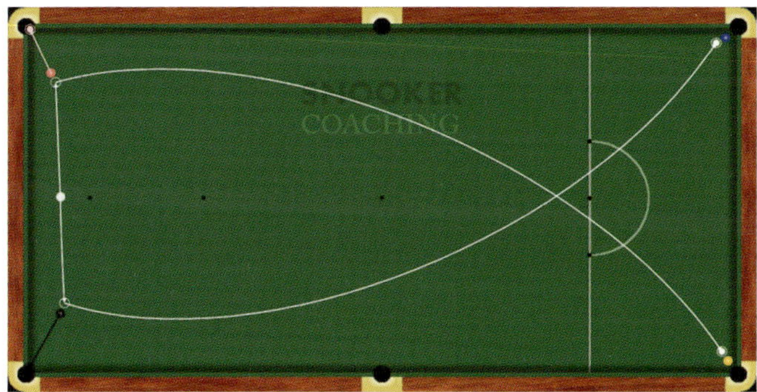

Why this Is a Good Exercise

1. Helps with generating power for deep screw shots
2. Improves knowledge of the movement of the white ball when hit with power
3. Increases confidence

Practice Objectives – Pot and Screw

Beginner	Pot pink and black 3 times each
Intermediate	Pot pink and yellow once
Advanced	Complete the exercise

Coaching Top Tips and Trivia

The elusive century break is beyond 99% or more of players, however the number of players claiming to have made a century break in the dim and distant past is surprisingly high – draw your own conclusion!

K89

RED TO BLACK WHEN WHITE IS OFF THE CUSHION

Stun to gain position on black

Description

Start from the position indicated with the red ball in a line with the black ball.
   From this position practise potting the red and stunning off the cushion for position on black.

Why this Is a Good Exercise

1. Very good practice in controlling the white ball
2. Good potting practice with red tight against the cushion
3. Improves break-building skills

Practice Objectives – Red to Black

Beginner   Complete pot on red and black once
Intermediate   Complete pot on red and black 3 times
Advanced   Complete pot on red and black 5 times

Coaching Top Tips and Trivia

The best advice for parents – try to stay well away from training and if possible from match play. Youngsters need to become independent and must be self-motivated. It's tough as you are doing the paying and the transporting, but it's essential for juniors to develop.

K90

LONG POT AND SCREW SHOT

Pot colour to top pocket and red to bottom pocket

Description

This is a challenging routine but one that can really sharpen your game up.

Set the balls as illustrated with a straight pot on yellow. Pot and screw back behind the baulk line and then pot a red.

Repeat on each colour and each red.

Remember it only counts if you pot and screw into baulk for your pot on red.

Why this Is a Good Exercise

1. Requires perfectly straight cueing
2. Encourages absolute stillness on the shot
3. Improves ability to screw the ball over distance

Practice Objectives – Long Pot and Screw Shot

Beginner   Pot colours down to blue
Intermediate   Pot each colour
Advanced   Complete the exercise

Coaching Top Tips and Trivia

Coaching is now a profession and as such coaches must be professional. Your coach should be well dressed and should keep records of what you have done and where you are up to in your programme.

Your coach should have a curriculum – if not consider your investment in coaching very carefully. Expect the highest of standard from your coach.

K91

TIGHT RED TO BLACK

Pot red and gain position on black

Description

Start from the position indicated with the red ball tight against the top cushion and the white up to one ball width off the cushion.

Play the pot on the red ball using top spin, which will bring the white off the side rail and back out for black.

Why this Is a Good Exercise

1. Very good practice for potting balls on the top cushion
2. Requires good touch and control
3. Increases break-building skills

Practice Objectives – Red to Black

Beginner   Complete pots on red and black once only
Intermediate   Complete pots on red and black 3 times
Advanced   Complete 5 times in succession

Coaching Top Tips and Trivia

I have found that a coach will love to give advice to a person who can already play but ignores someone who has absolutely no idea what they are doing. There is nothing more irritating as a professional coach than seeing one of your players targeted by another coach for reflected glory.

K92

A NIGHTMARE OF TRIANGLES

Clear the reds and then the colours

Description

Place the balls in small triangles as shown. Start from any position and start by potting all of the reds only. Once all of the reds are potted clear the colours in sequence.

Yes, this is a very tough one and certainly for the more advanced 100+ player, but it has been done on a number of occasions.

Why this Is a Good Exercise

1. Requires very high level of break-building skills
2. Improves very accurate cue ball control
3. Requires a high level of determination and concentration

Practice Objectives – Nightmare of Triangles

Beginner	Spend 15 minutes practising
Intermediate	Pot 5+ reds
Advanced	Complete the exercise

Coaching Top Tips and Trivia

For a talented junior to develop into a top player can take 10 years, so it's very important that juniors enjoy the experience and enjoy coaching sessions. Coaches must not be too serious and should keep lessons fun but structured. A self-motivated player does not need pushing!

K93

THREE-QUARTER-BALL SOFT STUN TO PINK

Gain position on pink off black

Description

Starting from the position indicated, which is a ¾ ball pot on the black ball, play a soft stun shot to gain good position on the pink ball.

Try to pot the pink and if you can, regain a ¾ ball pot on black.

Continue like this with as many loops as you can.

Why this Is a Good Exercise

1. Requires a good touch and control of a soft stun shot
2. Helps increase break-building skills
3. Improves consistency in and around the top end of the table

Practice Objectives – Stun to Pink

Beginner	Complete 1 full loop (black and pink)
Intermediate	Complete 2 full loops (black and pink)
Advanced	Complete 5 full loops (black and pink)

Coaching Top Tips and Trivia

There are players from nearly 50 countries participating in professional events with the strongest still being England. Given the numbers playing in China it's almost inevitable that in 10 years' time the strongest will be China.

K94

DEEP SCREW AND ARC SHOT

Split the reds and clear the table

Description

Pot the red positioned near the top pocket and screw into the triangle of reds, trying to split them into pottable positions. Clear the reds only to start with and on potting the last red gain position to clear colours in sequence.

Some luck involved with the initial split but after that its plain sailing.

Why this Is a Good Exercise

1. Improves control of the cue ball
2. Requires excellent cueing and a good follow-through
3. Buils up your break-building skills

Practice Objectives – Screw and Arc Shot

Beginner   Spend 15 minutes practising
Intermediate   Pot 4+ reds
Advanced   Complete the exercise

Coaching Top Tips and Trivia

There is absolutely nothing worse than seeing a player that is all technique but no natural flow. Technique is critical but you must never let it overshadow your natural ability or you will end up frustrated and hating the game. Stay natural but within a framework that allows you to play!

K95

FULL-BALL POT AND SCREW

Screw for position on the black ball

Description

Starting from the position indicated (full ball pot on pink) play the shot with screw to gain position on the black ball.

Try to also pot the black ball.

Why this Is a Good Exercise

1. Requires accurate potting and control
2. Improves ability to play screw shots
3. Increases break-building skills

Practice Objectives – Pot and Screw

Beginner	Pot pink and black once
Intermediate	Pot pink and black twice
Advanced	Pot pink and black 10 times in succession

Coaching Top Tips and Trivia

Compared to many sports the prize money in snooker is still low. If you are ranked outside of the top 50 in the world it's very hard to make a living given that the standard of the top ranked players is so high. Being a professional player is not easy by any means.

K96

NOT SO EASY CLEARANCE

Looks easy – not quite so!

Description

A nice simple clearance – it's not quite as easy as it looks, but no great problem to the advanced player.

Start by clearing all of the reds – then the colours in sequence – pretty easy apart from red near black and brown!

You can start from any position.

Why this Is a Good Exercise

1. Requires knowledge and accuracy
2. Improves pre-shot planning, as the exercise can't be done without it!
3. Needs persistence and concentration

Practice Objectives – Not So Easy Clearance

Beginner	Spend 15 minutes practising
Intermediate	Pot 5+ reds
Advanced	Complete the exercise

Coaching Top Tips and Trivia

A pause in the cueing from the final backswing to the delivery has become part of the game and is aimed at smoothing the delivery. All good, but if you have played for many years without a pause be careful about changing it because it can destroy your game. Better to just slow down your final backswing, it's safer and will not destroy your enjoyment.

K97

THREE-QUARTER-BALL POT TO MIDDLE

Gain position for the black ball

Description

Starting from the position indicated (¾ ball pot on pink) play the shot with stun to gain position on the black ball.

Try to also pot the black ball.

Why this Is a Good Exercise

1. Recognition of a ¾ ball pot to middle
2. Requires control and fluent cueing
3. Improves break-building skills

Practice Objectives – Pot to Middle

Beginner   Pot pink and black once
Intermediate   Pot pink and black twice
Advanced   Pot pink and black 10 times in succession

Coaching Top Tips and Trivia

The player who has made the most centuries on the biggest stage of all, the Crucible in Sheffield, is Ronnie O'Sullivan followed by Stephen Hendry. Quite remarkable, but it's almost inevitable that at some point in time a player will emerge who will go beyond even Ronnie's total – that is sport!

K98

SEE-SAW POTTING

Pot a red and then a colour and back to red

Description

Position the balls as illustrated with a line of reds at the top end of the table and the colours at the opposite end of the table.

Starting from any position on the reds pot a red gaining position on the yellow ball. Pot this and gain position on another red.

Repeat the sequence.

The colours must be cleared in sequence.

Why this Is a Good Exercise

1. Requires good potting and accurate control of the white ball
2. Improves judgement of pace
3. Increase knowledge of positional play

Practice Objectives – See-Saw Potting

Beginner	Pot 1 red and 1 colour
Intermediate	Pot 2 reds and 2 colours
Advanced	Complete the exercise

Coaching Top Tips and Trivia

To nominate a colour or not – that is the question.

You should nominate the colour, but in practice if it is obvious then players don't nominate and referees ignore the rule.

K99

THREE-QUARTER-BALL STUN SHOT OFF PINK TO BLACK

Stun for position on the black ball

Description

Starting from the position indicated (¾ ball pot on pink) play the shot with stun to gain position on the black ball.

Try to also pot the black ball.

Why this Is a Good Exercise

1. Improves control when using stun
2. Recognition of ¾ ball potting position
3. Increases break-building skills

Practice Objectives – Pink to Black

Beginner   Pot pink and black once
Intermediate   Pot pink and black twice
Advanced   Pot pink and black 10 times in succession

Coaching Top Tips and Trivia

The top snooker players do not win every match. Arguably the greatest ever, Stephen Hendry lost 33% of his professional matches, so for every three matches he played he lost one of them – something of a surprise to many people.

K100

FUN ON THE BLACK

Pot black by coming off 3 cushions

Description

Sometimes it's great just to have a bit of fun when you are at your club.

This particular trick shot is a favourite of many professionals and quite easy.

Use a bit of left-hand side and after a couple of practice runs you will have mastered this one.

To make it look even better add in a few extra balls as obstacles to create an even better effect.

Why this Is a Good Exercise

1. Improves your knowledge of using side
2. Good for understanding of angles
3. Its great fun and will amaze your friends

Practice Objectives – Fun on the Black

Beginner   Complete once
Intermediate   Master
Advanced   Master

Coaching Top Tips and Trivia

To keep your cue running parallel to the cloth hold the cue predominantly with your index finger. As the cue goes into backswing the other fingers gently open but remain in contact with the cue and guiding it.

K101

QUARTER-BALL PINK TO BLACK USING TOP SPIN

Gain position on black off side and top cushions

Description

Starting from the position indicated (¼ ball pot on pink) play the shot with top spin to gain position on the black ball by coming off the top cushion.
Try to also pot the black ball.

Why this Is a Good Exercise

1. Needs control off a ¼ ball pot played over distance
2. Improves understanding of thin pots
3. Increases break-building skills

Practice Objectives – Black Using Top Spin

Beginner   Pot pink and black once
Intermediate   Pot pink and black twice
Advanced   Pot pink and black 10 times in succession

Coaching Top Tips and Trivia

There are lots and lots of people who can play the game well but there are very few who play the game well and have taken the time to study and learn every aspect of the game. As important as being able to pot balls is an encyclopaedic knowledge of how to play every single shot from every position.

K102

TOP-SPIN CURVE SHOT

Position on red after potting black

Description

You can really enjoy this one and release all your inhibitions!

With black right over the top pocket hit the white ball hard with as much top spin as you can.

It's a fraction off full-ball contact and if you catch it correctly you will pot the black and arc round for position on the red.

Don't worry about technique – go for it!

Why this Is a Good Exercise

1. Just occasionally you do use this shot in a match
2. This is fun and frees up your cueing arm
3. It will amaze your snooker friends

Practice Objectives – Top-Spin Curve Shot

Beginner	Practice for 10 minutes
Intermediate	Complete once
Advanced	Master the shot

Coaching Top Tips and Trivia

The most naturally talented player will not, in this day and age compete, even at National level, if he/she has not, in addition to having good technique, learned and studied the individual shots and disciplines involved with the modern game.

K103

THREE-QUARTER-BALL PINK TO BLACK USING TOP SPIN

Gain position off the top cushion

Description

Starting from the position indicated (¾ ball pot on pink) play the shot with top spin to gain position on the black ball by coming off the top cushion.

Try to also pot the black ball.

Why this Is a Good Exercise

1. Requires control to gain a favourable position on black
2. Good practice using top spin
3. Good for break-building skills

Practice Objectives – Black Using Top Spin

Beginner   Pot pink and black once
Intermediate   Pot pink and black twice
Advanced   Pot pink and black 10 times in succession

Coaching Top Tips and Trivia

You, the coach, your parents, your friends never quite know how good you are until you are faced with certain defining moments in your career. Come through those successfully and you will amaze even yourself at how good you have become.

K104

COLOURS INTO THE D

Send each colour into the D

Description

Looks easy in principle but can you complete it without missing?

With pink on its spot, place the remaining colours either side as illustrated.

Starting with the white ball in any position and in-between pink and black spots, aim to send each colour into the D.

Why this Is a Good Exercise

1. Improves judgement of pace
2. Requires good cueing and a gentle touch
3. Improves focus and concentration

Practice Objectives – Colours in the D

Beginner   Complete the exercise
Intermediate   Complete the exercise
Advanced   Complete the exercise without missing

Coaching Top Tips and Trivia

Women can most certainly compete at the very highest levels of the game. There is no shortage of talent, but there is a shortage of players, and still many clubs are less than welcoming to youngsters playing on their tables.

K105

THREE-QUARTER-BALL PINK TO BLACK

Gain position on black off ¾ ball pot on pink

Description

Starting from the position indicated (¾ ball pot on pink) play the shot with top spin to gain position on the black ball.

Try to also pot the black ball.

Why this Is a Good Exercise

1. Improves control when using top spin and coming off a cushion
2. Helps break-building skills
3. Requires concentration and pre-shot planning

Practice Objectives – Pink to Black

Beginner   Pot pink and black once
Intermediate   Pot pink and black twice
Advanced   Pot pink and black 10 times in succession

Coaching Top Tips and Trivia

The great players do, of course, get nervous, but the nerves disappear when they start to play. The also-rans get nervous and these nerves stay throughout a match and have a detrimental effect upon performance.

K106

COLOUR CLEARANCE ROAD BLOCK

Clear the colours and avoid the reds

Description

Set the balls as illustrated with each pocket covered by a colour (red over yellow pocket) and black on its spot.

Place the remaining reds in the formation shown. These act as blocks making it hard to gain position.

Starting from any position aim to clear the colours over the pockets (red first then in sequence) and once complete try to then clear all of the remaining reds.

Why this Is a Good Exercise

1. Pinpoint accuracy required
2. Improves positional play and judgement of pace
3. Challenging and requires pre-shot planning

Practice Objectives – The Road Block

Beginner	Pot colours down to green
Intermediate	Clear the colours
Advanced	Clear the colours and the reds

Coaching Top Tips and Trivia

To clarify – if a ball drops or falls into a pocket yet has not been struck but has moved due to vibration then the referee should replace the ball.

K107

AWKWARD CUEING PRACTICE

5 Straight reds from both sides of the table

Description

Starting from a straight position on each shot aim to pot the 5 straight reds into the middle pocket.

Complete 5 pots from each side of the table. You will need to shorten your grip, put your bridge hand on the back cushion and raise the butt slightly so you are slightly striking down.

Make a positive strike of the cue ball and stay down on the shot keeping your head still.

Why this Is a Good Exercise

1. Requires excellent cueing
2. Needs concentration
3. Encourages you to stay still on the shot

Practice Objectives – Cueing Practice

Beginner   Complete 5 pots
Intermediate   Complete 5 pots
Advanced   Complete 10 pots without missing

Coaching Top Tips and Trivia

Take your practice game into the match arena. You simply must practise with the intensity that you need in matchplay and your game must not differ. The best players can disregard their opponent and simply try to deliver in matchplay what they do in practice.

K108

MIDDLE POCKET ARC SHOT

Pot the black and arc the white into the middle pocket

Description

Looks tough but it's quite possible with some practice to master this one.

Set the black ball in an easy potting position for the top pocket.

Using a deep screw shot really hit through the ball to pot black and arc the white ball into the middle pocket as shown.

Cue power required!

Why this Is a Good Exercise

1. Improves control when playing deep screw
2. Liberating and fun – go for it!
3. A good little trick shot to amaze your friends with

Practice Objectives – Middle Pocket Arc Shot

Beginner   Just pot black and try to screw the ball
Intermediate   Complete once
Advanced   Complete 5 times

Coaching Top Tips and Trivia

The red balls are placed in a triangular frame in order to set them up correctly hence a single game of snooker is often referred to as a frame of snooker.

K109

BLACK BREAK-BUILDING EXERCISE

Improve your break-building skills around the black ball area

Description

Starting from position 1 aim to pot red/black combinations and try to clear the table.
Once completed repeat but this time starting from position 2.
The oval shapes indicate the ideal position for the cue ball to finish in order to pot black.

Why this Is a Good Exercise

1. Requires pre-shot planning
2. Improves positional play
3. Increases break-building skills in a confined area

Practice Objectives – Break-Building Exercise

Beginner   2 reds and 1 black
Intermediate   4 reds and 3 blacks
Advanced   2 clearances from each start position

Coaching Top Tips and Trivia

As a professional coach I encourage even the most talented juniors to be involved with many sports not just snooker. In the end the junior that loves the game and wants to go further in it will decide for themselves which is their favoured activity and which to devote their time to.

K110

EASY WARM-UP ROUTINE

Pot as many reds as you can

Description

Useful little warm-up routine to get the cue arm going before a match.
 Starting from any position aim to clear the reds in any order.
 Try to hit gently and smoothly and this will set you up for the match ahead.

Why this Is a Good Exercise

1. Good as a warm-up before a match
2. Encourages you to pot gently
3. Removes pre-match nerves or at least helps to calm them

Practice Objectives – Warm-Up Routine

Beginner   Pot 5+ reds
Intermediate   Pot 8+ reds
Advanced   Clear the table

Coaching Top Tips and Trivia

It is most definitely a foul shot if the cue ball jumps over an obstructing ball to hit
the object ball or any other ball.
 The jump shot is strictly reserved for the trick shot arena!

K111

QUARTER-BALL SAFETY SHOT

Safety into baulk

Description

Strike the cue ball with top spin to make approximately a ¼ ball contact or less with the red.

The aim is to get the cue ball tight to the baulk cushion without hitting any other balls in the process.

Practise from both sides of the table.

Why this Is a Good Exercise

1. Increases knowledge of safety play
2. Good practice for thin contact over distance
3. Excellent cueing required

Practice Objectives – Safety Shot

Beginner	Spend 15 minutes practising
Intermediate	Complete within 2 inches of baulk cushion × 3
Advanced	Complete within 2 inches of baulk cushion × 10

Coaching Top Tips and Trivia

With most sports prior to playing you warm-up and snooker should be the same. Develop your own little easy warm-up routine that you can use every time before you play. It builds confidence, gets the cue arm going and settles the nerves.

K112

RIGHT-HAND-SIDE BREAKER

Use side to go in-between blue and pink

Description

Here is a break-off shot that you are unlikely to use in a match but it may amuse your friends in the club.

With the white ball almost touching yellow use left-hand side to go in-between blue and pink and catch the end red to return to baulk.

Effective and enjoyable.

Why this Is a Good Exercise

1. Builds confidence and it's fun
2. Improves your ability to make a thin contact when using side over distance
3. Can throw your opponent off his game

Practice Objectives – Side Breaker

Beginner	Practise this for 10 minutes
Intermediate	Complete once
Advanced	Complete once and within 1 inch of cushion

Coaching Top Tips and Trivia

When you start to play in higher standard competitions, be aware of the dress code as this can be strict and is enforced by the referees.

Players will often wear something they have never played in before and this can be off-putting – practise in what you play matches in.

K113

HALF-BALL BLUE TO PINK USING BOTTOM AND LEFT

Gain position on pink by going between brown and yellow

Description

Pot the ½ ball blue to the middle using bottom left to gain position on the pink ball by coming off bottom and side cushions.

Try to also pot the pink ball.

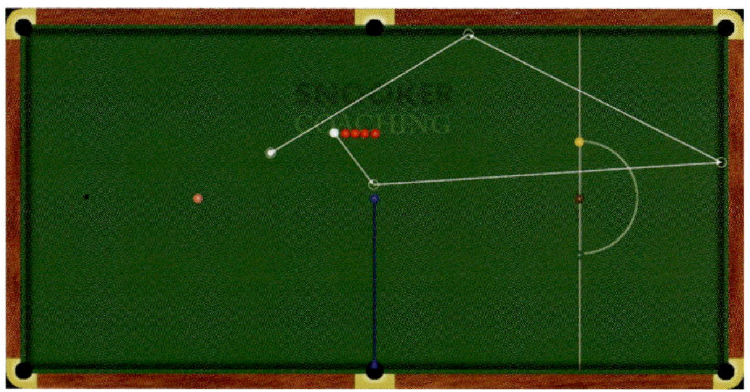

Why this Is a Good Exercise

1. Excellent practice in avoiding baulk colours
2. Increases knowledge of the use of side
3. Requires considerable practice

Practice Objectives – Bottom and Left

Beginner   Complete 10 pots on blue
Intermediate   Complete 10 pots on blue and 5 on pink
Advanced   Complete 10 sets of blue and pink

Coaching Top Tips and Trivia

Look for a practising coach who not only talks the talk but who has a big clientele of juniors and adults and who coaches as a profession. Many people talk about coaching and sell advice but few have the skills to build a business from actually coaching in numbers.

K114

TOP-SPIN ARC TO MIDDLE

Pot black and white in one shot

Description

Using plenty of cue power and lots of top spin pot the black into the top pocket
and let the white ball arc into the middle pocket.

The reds grouped next to the middle will assist the white ball to go in the pocket.
This is great fun so let your cue arm and talent flow.

Why this Is a Good Exercise

1. Good to have in your trick shot repertoire
2. Improves ability to split balls and continue a break
3. Great fun to practise

Practice Objectives – Arc to Middle

Beginner   Pot the black with top spin 3 times
Intermediate   Complete once
Advanced   Complete 5 times

Coaching Top Tips and Trivia

Snooker players are, in the main, the most honest people you will ever meet. Most
players will call their own fouls and even if a hair of the hand touches a ball and
nobody has seen it most players will call a foul on themselves.

K115

HALF-BALL SAFETY SHOT

Back to the bottom cushion

Description

Strike the cue ball with top spin to make approximately a ½ ball contact with the red.

The aim is to get the cue ball tight to the baulk cushion without hitting any other balls in the process.

Practise from both sides of the table.

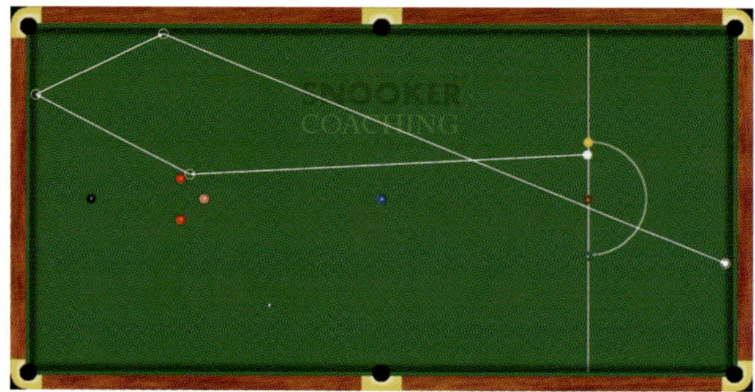

Why this Is a Good Exercise

1. Helps develop correct contact on object ball when playing safe over distance
2. Requires careful aiming
3. Requires good cueing

Practice Objectives – Safety Shot

Beginner   Spend 15 minutes practising
Intermediate   Complete within 2 inches of baulk cushion × 3
Advanced   Complete within 2 inches of baulk cushion × 10

Coaching Top Tips and Trivia

Before your practice session or your match always iron the table to get a little speed into the cloth. Slow cloths are the greatest equalizers that there are as even top professionals can struggle to break-build on a dead slow cloth.

K116

GREEN POCKET ARC SHOT

Pot black and white to green pocket

Description

A most satisfying shot when you manage to pull this one off.

Pot the black into the top pocket using a lot of top spin to arc the white ball into the green pocket.

Some experimenting is required to get the ideal start position and plenty of cue power!

Why this Is a Good Exercise

1. Improves positional play using power and spin
2. Requires good cueing
3. It's fun and a challenge

Practice Objectives – Green Pocket Arc

Beginner   Pot the black with top spin 3 times
Intermediate   Complete once
Advanced   Complete 3 times

Coaching Top Tips and Trivia

A free ball is when a player is snookered on the reds following a foul shot from his opponent. He may then nominate any colour as a red ball. Once potted the red counts as one point and a colour is then nominated in the usual way.

K117

HALF-BALL BLUE TO PINK

In and out of baulk using left-hand side

Description

Pot the ½ ball blue to the middle using left-hand side to check the white ball off the bottom cushion for position on pink to top pocket.

You will need about 60% power for this shot dependent upon the table/cloth you are on.

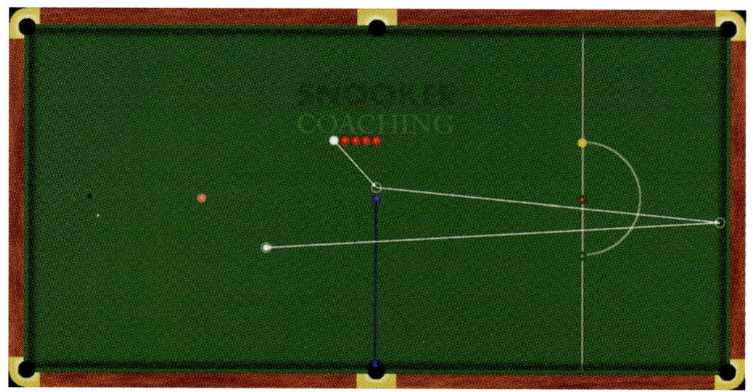

Why this Is a Good Exercise

1. Increases the understanding of using side off a ½ ball pot
2. Develops touch over a long distance positional shot
3. Excellent potting practice

Practice Objectives – Blue to Pink

Beginner   Complete 10 pots on blue
Intermediate   Complete 10 pots on blue and 5 on pink
Advanced   Complete 10 sets of blue and pink

Coaching Top Tips and Trivia

There is a trend to having a greater bend in the bridge hand arm than in previous years. Too big a bend is not natural, so extend your arm without it being ramrod straight and rigid. A natural extension of the arm puts a little tension in the sails and is generally the position most professionals adopt.

K118

REVERSE BREAK

Make a 50+ break

Description

Place the balls as illustrated.
   The value of the colours remains the same as usual.
   The challenge is to make a break from this unfamiliar position.
   Anything above 50 and you are doing well.

Why this Is a Good Exercise

1. Helps you cope with unfamiliar patterns of play
2. Challenging and requires a lot of pre-shot planning
3. Helps develop break-building skills

Practice Objectives – Reverse Break

Beginner   Make a 10+ break
Intermediate   Make a 20+ break
Advanced   Make a 50+ break

Coaching Top Tips and Trivia

Beware that with a free ball and unless only pink and black remain a player is not allowed to snooker his opponent behind the ball he nominates. If only pink and black remain then you can snooker your opponent behind the nominated free ball.

K119

HALF-BALL BLUE TO PINK USING STUN

Stun shot for position on pink to top pocket

Description

Pot the ½ ball blue to the middle using stun to come off the top cushion gaining position on the pink ball.

You can establish the ½ ball position by starting with a red ball in a straight line with the blue then placing 3 other reds next to it. Then place your white ball and it's in a ½ ball pot for blue to middle.

Try to also pot the pink ball.

Why this Is a Good Exercise

1. Improves control over stun shots
2. Increases understanding of the movement of the white ball
3. Increases knowledge of ½ ball potting

Practice Objectives – Pink Using Stun

Beginner   Complete 10 pots on blue
Intermediate   Complete 10 pots on blue and 5 on pink
Advanced   Complete 10 sets of blue and pink

Coaching Top Tips and Trivia

The first ever maximum break (147) made in the World Snooker Championships was by Cliff Thorburn in 1983.

K120

DEVELOP YOUR TOUCH

From baulk line to pocket in over 100 shots

Description

Start with the white ball on the baulk line.

The aim of the exercise is to try to make at least 100 shots before your white ball drops in the yellow pocket.

You need a delicate touch and steady nerves to achieve this.

It's possible to do this in over 1000 shots!

Why this Is a Good Exercise

1. Develops touch
2. Improves awareness of how close your tip is to the cue ball
3. Its great fun to try

Practice Objectives – Develop Your Touch

Beginner   In over 20 shots
Intermediate   In over 50 shots
Advanced   In over 100+ shots

Coaching Top Tips and Trivia

Three consecutive misses from an un-snookered position means the immediate forfeit of the game – at least it does at a high level of the game; however, it's not enforced in club play.

K121

HALF-BALL BLUE TO PINK USING TOP SPIN

Half-ball pot gaining position on pink

Description

Pot the ½ ball blue to the middle using top-spin to gain position on the pink ball.

You can establish the ½ ball position by starting with a red ball in a straight line with the blue then placing 3 other reds next to it. Then place your white ball and it's in a ½ ball pot for blue to middle.

Try to also pot the pink ball.

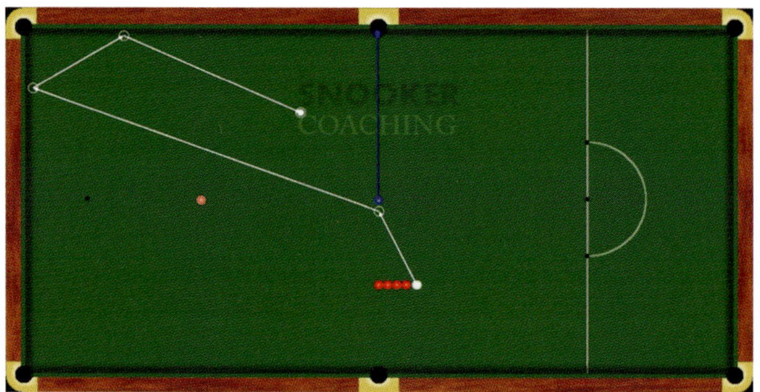

Why this Is a Good Exercise

1. Increases understanding of the movement of the white ball
2. Excellent ½ ball potting practice
3. Good for break-building when slightly out of position

Practice Objectives – Pink Using Top

Beginner   Complete 10 pots on blue
Intermediate   Complete 10 pots on blue and 5 on pink
Advanced   Complete 10 sets of blue and pink

Coaching Top Tips and Trivia

The first ever UK Championships was held in 1977 and was won by Patsy Fagan.

The winner's cheque was for the grand sum of £2000, which doesn't sound like a lot now, but was a fortune for a few days' work back then.

K122

GIVE ME A BREAK

Get as high a break as you can

Description

Position the balls as illustrated and starting from any position aim to make as high a break as you can.

For the experienced player this is a fairly easy routine, however it requires concentration for about 10 minutes.

Why this Is a Good Exercise

1. Builds confidence in break-building
2. Requires you to concentrate for about 10 minutes
3. Improves pre-shot planning

Practice Objectives – Give Me a Break

Beginner	Score a 10+ break
Intermediate	Score a 25+ break
Advanced	Make at least 50+ break

Coaching Top Tips and Trivia

There are many components that go into what could be described as perfect technique. If you have paid for coaching lessons then there is simply no reason why an able bodied person should not have a very good technique with virtually everything conforming to standard practice.

K123

CONSECUTIVE PINKS

Aim to pot as many pinks as you can

Description

Pot the pink ball as shown and leave the cue ball on the line of the shot for the next pot.

Re-spot the pink and continue to pot the pink again.

Use all cushions and the pockets indicated.

Pot as many pinks as you can without missing.

Why this Is a Good Exercise

1. Accurate positional play needed
2. Shot planning needed
3. Concentration required

Practice Objectives – Consecutive Pinks

Beginner   3 pinks
Intermediate   6 pinks
Advanced   12+ pinks

Coaching Top Tips and Trivia

Walter Lindrum and a small number of other top players became so good at the game that billiards became the only game to perish because the players were so good at it.

K124

REDS TO MIDDLE

Pot reds into the middle pocket

Description

Place a red on the pink spot and 3 reds either side and about 1 ball-width apart.
   Place the white ball as shown on the bottom red and just off a full-ball pot.
   Play a soft screw shot potting the red and pot with a soft screw gaining position
on the next red for a similar shot.

Why this Is a Good Exercise

1. Accurate aiming required
2. Pre-shot planning needed
3. Tight control of the cue ball needed

Practice Objectives – Reds to Middle

Beginner   2 consecutive pots
Intermediate   4 consecutive pots
Advanced   Clear the line without missing

Coaching Top Tips and Trivia

There are simply no short cuts to success and there has never been a player who
could just pick up a cue and knock in a big break. Hours, days, weeks and years
are required to become proficient regardless of how much ability you possess.

K125

THREE-QUARTER-BALL THROUGH THE LINE

Find the gap and pot the black

Description

Pot the ¾ ball blue using the relevant spin to gain position on the black ball, avoiding the marker balls on the way through.

Pot the black and repeat, gaining position by going through each gap in the line.

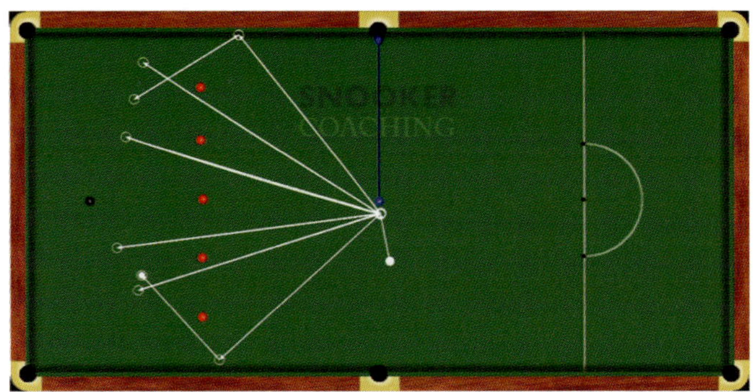

Why this Is a Good Exercise

1. Increases knowledge of which spins to use
2. Increases your ability to judge pace
3. Excellent ¾ ball potting practice

Practice Objectives – Through the Line

Beginner	Spend 30 minutes trying this exercise
Intermediate	Complete the exercise
Advanced	Complete the exercise in under 20 shots

Coaching Top Tips and Trivia

Practice clearing the colours and start from various positions. Even in the amateur ranks the top players will clear the colours 9 times out of 10 and in the professional ranks they simply have to.

Aim for 3 full clearances in succession.

K126

HALF-BALL CENTRE TOP

Pot and over the pink spot

Description

Pot the half-ball black hitting the white centre ball. The white ball will, if struck correctly, bounce off the bottom rail and roll over the pink spot.

Why this Is a Good Exercise

1. Increases knowledge of trajectory
2. Excellent half-ball potting practice
3. Good for judgement of pace

Practice Objectives – Centre Top

Beginner   Spend 15 minutes practising
Intermediate   Spend 30 minutes practising
Advanced   Complete 30 times

Coaching Top Tips and Trivia

Try giving and receiving a 120 start to your opponent. If you have to make 120 points you know you have to try your hardest and if you receive 120 you know that you must not lose the game.

This sort of practice applies pressure and sharpens your game up.

K127

HALF-BALL BELOW CENTRE 45-DEGREE BOUNCE

Half-ball pot off top cushion

Description

Pot the half-ball black striking below the centre of the cue ball.

The cue ball will, if struck correctly, bounce off the top rail at a 45 degree angle going between the side rail and pink spot as illustrated.

Why this Is a Good Exercise

1. Excellent half-ball potting practice
2. Increases knowledge of trajectory
3. Increases judgement of pace

Practice Objectives – 45 Degree Bounce

Beginner	Spend 15 minutes practising
Intermediate	Spend 30 minutes practising
Advanced	Complete 30 times

Coaching Top Tips and Trivia

You might be a World Champion but this game is cruel – if you don't play or practise you will lose to amateurs.

Once you start as a pro you don't stop practising for the duration of your career, so it's not for everyone!

K128

HALF-BALL RUNNING SIDE POT

Half-ball pot off top and side cushions

Description

Pot the half-ball black with a stun shot striking low on the cue ball and with running side.

The cue ball will bounce off the top and side cushions as shown in the diagram.

Why this Is a Good Exercise

1. Knowledge of the use of running side
2. Judgement of pace
3. Knowledge of angles

Practice Objectives – Running Side Pot

Beginner   Spend 15 minutes practising
Intermediate   Spend 30 minutes practising
Advanced   Complete 30 times

Coaching Top Tips and Trivia

Practise concentrating.

Start by staring at a snooker ball and nothing else for 1 minute. Build this up until you can focus on a ball for 15 minutes without letting anything distract you.

K129

ADVANCED LONG POTTING ANGLES

Pot and stun for black from 10 angles

Description

Place 10 reds in a line equally spaced from the green spot down to just past the pink spot.

Start with a full-ball pot on the red and stun for position on the black.

Repeat from every position marked by the reds and placing the object ball in a full-ball pot with the cue ball each time.

The further you move up the table the more you will need to lengthen the cue and hit lower down on the white to stun for black.

Why this Is a Good Exercise

1. Need straight and accurate cueing
2. Improves stun shot control over varying distances
3. Great potting practice

Practice Objectives – Long Potting Angles

Beginner	Spend 30 minutes practising
Intermediate	Complete the exercise
Advanced	Complete in under 20 shots

Coaching Top Tips and Trivia

The Barbican – the outer defence of a castle or walled city, especially a double tower above a gate or drawbridge.

K130

THE GREAT ESCAPE

Hit each red from below the black spot

Description

Place the balls as indicated with the colours on their spots and the reds positioned in-between.

Starting with the white ball positioned in-between the top cushion and the black ball aim to come off the side cushion and contact each red ball.

Start with the red that's in-between the black and pink balls and work down the line until you have contacted each red.

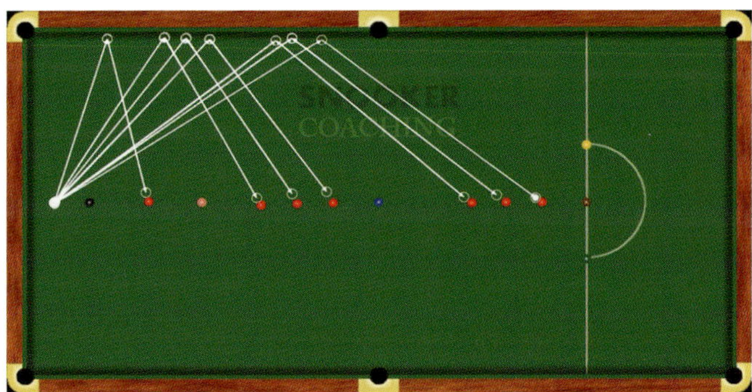

Why this Is a Good Exercise

1. Increases your understanding of angles and escaping from snookers
2. Requires concentration and persistence
3. Makes you a better and more knowledgeable player

Practice Objectives – The Great Escape

Beginner   Spend 30 minutes practising
Intermediate   Complete the exercise
Advanced   Complete once without missing

Coaching Top Tips and Trivia

The word 'hustler' was in use in the USA as early as 1825 and referred to a pick-pocket. Now used in snooker to describe a player who induces others less skilled to play for high stakes.

K131

BOTTOM CUSHION ESCAPES

Escape from side to bottom cushion

Description

Place the reds as indicated on the bottom cushion and the white ball on the black spot.

You must come off the side cushion to make contact with each red in turn starting with the red that is nearest to the yellow pocket.

Play at a slow to medium pace so that the cushion does not alter your estimated escape.

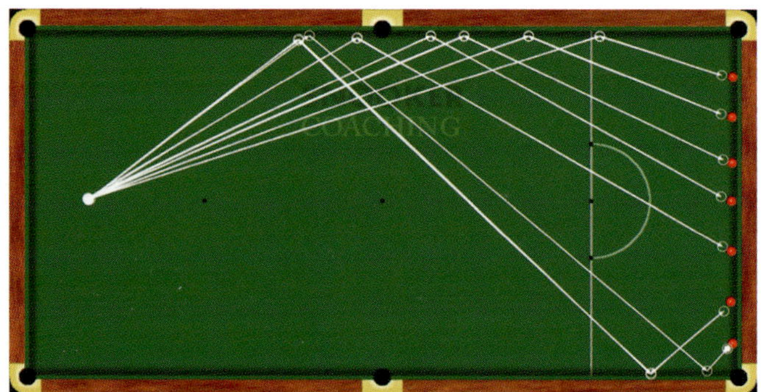

Why this Is a Good Exercise

1. Increases understanding of escaping from a snooker
2. Improves understanding of the strength a shot needs to be played when escaping from a snooker
3. Greater understanding of angles

Practice Objectives – Cushion Escapes

Beginner	Spend 30 minutes practising
Intermediate	Complete the exercise
Advanced	Complete once without missing

Coaching Top Tips and Trivia

A mace was an early form of a cue and had a solid wooden head with a flat face, which was attached to a wooden handle. The mace could be shoved along the table in order to propel the billiard ball on the intended path.

K132

ESCAPE TO THE COLOURS

From brown spot to side and contact each colour

Description

Place the colours in order across the table as illustrated.

Starting with the white ball on the brown spot aim to come off the side cushion and contact each colour in sequence starting of course with yellow.

Use the minimum pace you can.

Try to complete the six escapes without missing.

Why this Is a Good Exercise

1. Improves knowledge and understanding of escaping from snookers
2. Improves understanding of angles
3. Great to improve your ability to play an escape at the correct and minimum pace

Practice Objectives – Escapes

Beginner	Spend 30 minutes practising
Intermediate	Complete the exercise
Advanced	Complete once without missing

Coaching Top Tips and Trivia

The 'masse' shot involves the extreme application of side. It is achieved by raising the butt of the cue, allowing a player to strike the cue ball from above.

K133

THE MACHINE-GUN SHOT

Have some fun and a break from training

Description

Place the balls as illustrated along the baulk line with about 2 inches distance between them ensuring each ball will pot into the corner pocket.

Place the cue ball in a position where it will pot into the corner pocket.

Strike the cue ball first with the aim of potting all of the other balls first before the cue ball enters the same pocket.

Why this Is a Good Exercise

1. It's great fun!
2. Helps you relax and forget about technique
3. One to impress your friends with

Practice Objectives – Machine-Gun Shot

Beginner   Spend 30 minutes practising
Intermediate   Complete the exercise
Advanced   Complete 3 times in succession

Coaching Top Tips and Trivia

Which is the top and which is the bottom end of the table? It's amazing that a person can play the game for 50 years and still not know, but it's true that most people think that the bottom end of the table is near the black spot, which is of course wrong.

K134

TRICKERY WITH THE BLACK BALL

Pot black to middle

Description

A trick shot often performed by professional players at exhibitions as it's not one that's easy for the average player.

The black ball is placed on the pink spot with the two groups of three reds surrounding and touching each other.

Use power and deep screw to strike the nearest red.

Hopefully the black will be deflected off the furthest away red into the middle pocket.

Why this Is a Good Exercise

1. A good one to impress your friends with
2. Requires accuracy and power
3. Great fun!

Practice Objectives – Trickery

Beginner	Spend 10 minutes practising
Intermediate	Complete the shot
Advanced	Complete the shot

Coaching Top Tips and Trivia

A 'cue man' used to be the man who looked after the club members' cues. He would ensure the cues had good tips on them and that they were clean and in good condition.

K135

IMPOSSIBLE BLACK TO MIDDLE

Amaze your friends by potting a seemingly impossible black to middle

Description

Place the balls as illustrated ensuring that the three reds and the black are touching each other and are tight against the cushion.

For this shot, a favourite of many pro-players, you need to strike low and firm ensuring you contact the first red dead centre or the shot will not work.

The leading red strikes the red to the side leaving a path for black to hit the red over the middle and go in off.

Why this Is a Good Exercise

1. It's fun!
2. Builds confidence
3. Amazes your friends

Practice Objectives – Black to Middle

Beginner   Spend 10 minutes practising
Intermediate   Complete the trick shot
Advanced   Complete the trick shot

Coaching Top Tips and Trivia

Deflection is the description for the bend that occurs in the shaft of a cue as the tip makes contact with the cue ball.

K136

AS SEEN ON TV

4 cushion pot

Description

This shot is one of the professional player's favourite party pieces.

It looks good and is a reliable trick shot on which to finish the evening on a high note.

No great secret to this one.

Strike the cue ball at 5 o'clock and nice and firm sending the black ball off 4 cushions and into the top pocket.

Why this Is a Good Exercise

1. Needs straight and accurate cueing
2. Increases understanding of angles
3. Great fun and will amaze your friends

Practice Objectives – As Seen on TV

Beginner	Spend 10 minutes practising
Intermediate	Complete the exercise
Advanced	Complete the exercise

Coaching Top Tips and Trivia

The demand for ivory in the manufacture of billiard balls was so high that a reward was offered for the discovery of a substitute. This led to John Hyatt developing a ball made of celluloid.

K137

THREE REDS FROM ONE SHOT

Amaze the crowd with 3 reds from one shot

Description

Not the easiest trick shot but a great one when it comes off.

Place balls as illustrated but ensure that the red next to black is a fraction off the cushion and touching black.

For this shot use strong left-hand side playing off the black to travel round 3 cushions to pot the red over the yellow pocket. The black moves forward to pot the red over top and the other red goes in the middle.

Why this Is a Good Exercise

1. Great fun and very impressive when it works
2. Increases your confidence to perform on the stage
3. Helps your understanding of angles

Practice Objectives – Three Reds

Beginner	Spend 10 minutes practising
Intermediate	Complete the shot
Advanced	Complete the shot

Coaching Top Tips and Trivia

The snooker ladder is a means of determining a players ranking, normally within a club. Players are listed in sequence and a player may challenge the one immediately above himself on the list. If he/she wins then the positions are reversed.

K138

HARD 3s FOR 10 MINUTES

Easy in principle!

Description

One of my favourite routines as in principle it's easy but in practice only the best players can do it.

Set a timer for 10 minutes and start with red/black/red. Re-spot and move on to the red/blue/red combination. Re-spot and complete red/brown/red combination

Continue in this loop without missing for 10 minutes. You can start from any position you think is best for each combination.

Why this Is a Good Exercise

1. Requires excellent concentration
2. Improves close range positional play
3. Great potting practice

Practice Objectives – Hard 3s

Beginner	Spend 30 minutes practising
Intermediate	Spend 30 minutes practising
Advanced	Complete the exercise – no misses!

Coaching Top Tips and Trivia

The nap of the cloth is a directional pile in the cloth. Playing with the nap means a ball is rolling up the table, and against the nap is a ball going down the table towards the baulk end.

K139

15 RED WARM-UP ROUTINE

Clear the table and get the cue arm moving freely

Description

Place the reds as illustrated and all in easy potting positions.

Starting from any position aim to clear all of the reds without missing.

Take care, when potting the object ball, not to disturb any of the other balls as doing so makes it much harder to clear the table.

Concentrate!

Why this Is a Good Exercise

1. Builds confidence but requires concentration
2. Improves control and positional play
3. Great potting practice

Practice Objectives – 15 Reds

Beginner	Spend 30 minutes practising
Intermediate	Complete the exercise
Advanced	Complete 3 times in succession

Coaching Top Tips and Trivia

The bend in the arm is an interesting topic. Joe Davis suggested that the bridge hand arm should be ramrod straight whereas modern players sometimes have a pronounced bend in the arm. My advice is to extend the arm until you feel slight resistance – that's the correct and best position.

K140

ADVANCED 3s COLOUR CLEARANCE

Pot 2 reds and a colour in sequence

Description

Place the balls as illustrated with 2 reds either side of each of the colours.

Start by potting each of the reds either side of yellow and then pot the yellow ball gaining position for the reds either side of the green ball.

Continue clearing the 2 reds then the colour in sequence.

This is far from easy and requires at least one cannon to complete the sequence.

Why this Is a Good Exercise

1. Needs accurate positional play and good touch
2. Improves pre-shot planning particularly when on the red/brown combination
3. Very good for improving break-building skills

Practice Objectives – Advanced 3s

Beginner	Spend 30 minutes practising
Intermediate	Complete the exercise
Advanced	Complete the exercise twice in succession

Coaching Top Tips and Trivia

These days there are all sorts of gadgets and gimmicks that are claimed help you to improve. Speaking as a working coach I say the best way to improve is good technique and a well-constructed programme of practice and learning – there are no short cuts!

K141

SOFT SCREW-SHOT TRAINING

Pot black into the top pocket and screw into first red

Description

Place the balls as illustrated with a reverse triangle of 6 reds and black on its spot.

Using a soft screw shot pot black and gently split the reds into open potting positions.

After potting black go on to pot each of the red balls to make a 13 break.

Use minimum pace to achieve a good split.

Why this Is a Good Exercise

1. Requires a good pot and accuracy to hit the first red and achieve a split
2. Improves control and understanding of the correct pace needed
3. Increases ability to concentrate and focus

Practice Objectives – Soft Screw Shot

Beginner	Spend 30 minutes practising
Intermediate	Complete the exercise
Advanced	Complete the exercise within 20 minutes

Coaching Top Tips and Trivia

Snooker is enjoying worldwide popularity and as such big names in advertising; however, the first TV sponsorship was from Super Crystalate way back in 1977.

K142

SMALL LINE AND COLOURS

Make as high a break as you can

Description

Place the balls as illustrated with the colours on their spots and 5 reds evenly spread in-between the pink and black spots.

Starting from any position pot a red and go on to make as high a break as you can.

Although seemingly easy this requires skill and concentration and it's a very good indicator as to where you are in skill terms.

Why this Is a Good Exercise

1. Excellent to improve break-building skills
2. A good indicator of your current level of skill
3. Great potting practice

Practice Objectives – Small Line

Beginner   Spend 30 minutes practising
Intermediate   Spend 30 minutes practising and note best break
Advanced   Complete at least 1 full clearance

Coaching Top Tips and Trivia

The ladies game is growing fast both in popularity and standard of play. The first ladies world champion was Vera Selby back in 1976.

5 THREES AND A BLACK

Pot all of the reds and finish with the black

Description

Place the balls as illustrated with the reds in easy potting positions and black near the top pocket.

This is a good warm-up exercise but requires concentration even though it is easy.

Starting from any position aim to pot each group of 3 reds and finish by gaining good position on the black, which you pot to complete the exercise.

Why this Is a Good Exercise

1. Very good warm-up routine that builds confidence
2. Improves positional play and concentration
3. Builds confidence

Practice Objectives – 5s and 3s

Beginner   Spend 15 minutes practising
Intermediate   Complete the exercise
Advanced   Complete 3 times without missing

Coaching Top Tips and Trivia

Ken Doherty was the first player to become world amateur and professional champion.

K144

ADVANCED WARM-UP

Easy break to get the cue arm moving

Description

Place the balls as illustrated with 3 groups of reds and yellow, green and brown on their spots.

Aim to pot all of the reds, which in itself is not easy, but from the final red gain position to clear the colours in the usual sequence.

This is a great warm-up to use before a match as it is fun and builds your confidence prior to playing.

Why this Is a Good Exercise

1. Very good pre-match warm-up routine
2. Improves break-building skills and requires relaxation and concentration
3. Great potting practice

Practice Objectives – Warm-up

Beginner   Spend 10 minutes practising
Intermediate   Complete the exercise in 10 minutes
Advanced   Complete in under 5 minutes

Coaching Top Tips and Trivia

The first time that opponents in a game of billiards made successive four figure breaks occurred when the genius of both Walter Lindrum and Joe Davis met in 1932. Walter made his highest break of 4137 followed by Joe with a break of 1247.

K145

DEAD RED BACK TO BAULK WHITE

A good safety to know

Description

Place a red tight against the top cushion below the black spot and the cue ball on the brown spot.

Hit red full in the face and you will hopefully send white back off red and into baulk for a good safety shot.

If you don't hit red full in the face you will find this exercise hard.

Why this Is a Good Exercise

1. When there are limited options for safety it's a good shot to know
2. Increases your understanding of available options
3. Good fun to practise and know

Practice Objectives – Dead Red

Beginner   Spend 10 minutes practising
Intermediate   Complete the exercise
Advanced   Complete 3 times in succession

Coaching Top Tips and Trivia

The spider-rest, with its arched legs that can slide over a ball, was originally known as the high arch rest.

K146

TIGHT CONTROL BREAK

Clear the table from a congested position

Description

Place the balls as illustrated ensuring black can be potted to both top pockets.

Aim to make as high a break as you can but you can only pot the reds into the top pockets.

Once you have potted all of the reds with colours clear the colours in sequence.

This is a challenging exercise requiring very accurate positional play.

Why this Is a Good Exercise

1. Needs accurate positional play
2. Improves control when space is limited
3. Realistic and a good measure of your skill level

Practice Objectives – Tight Control

Beginner	Spend 30 minutes practising
Intermediate	Spend 30 minutes practising
Advanced	Complete full clearance

Coaching Top Tips and Trivia

All on the black refers to a situation where players' scores differ by fewer than 7 points. If the difference in points is exactly 7 and a player pots the black to tie, then the black is re-spotted for a sudden death finish.

K147

REALISTIC LINE BREAK

Make as high a break as you can

Description

Place the balls as illustrated.

This exercise is a more realistic variation on the line of balls, which is a standard practice routine.

Starting from any position aim to make as high a break as you can.

The irregular position of the reds reflects a more realistic position than a straight line of balls.

Why this Is a Good Exercise

1. Good for improving break-building skills
2. Realistic and challenging but also fun
3. Increases ability to concentrate and good for building confidence

Practice Objectives – Line Break

Beginner	Spend 30 minutes practising
Intermediate	Spend 30 minutes practising
Advanced	Complete clearance

Coaching Top Tips and Trivia

Where will the game be in the years to come?

Given the huge interest and volume of players from China it looks to be a certainty that in the years to come the world championship trophy will be held by a Chinese player.

THE COMPLETE BOOK OF
SNOOKER
SHOTS
David Horrix